HARRISBURG
AND THE
CIVIL WAR

HARRISBURG
AND THE
CIVIL WAR

Defending the Keystone of the Union

COOPER H. WINGERT

Foreword by Richard J. Sommers, PhD

THE
History
PRESS

Published by The History Press
Charleston, SC 29403
www.historypress.net

Cover images: Front: "The Capitol Grounds at Harrisburg turned into a camp," *Harper's Weekly*, October 4, 1862. *Dickinson College Archives and Special Collections*; *View of Harrisburg. Penn.*, 1855 lithograph. *Historical Society of Dauphin County*. Back: Brigadier General Joseph F. Knipe (inset). *MOLLUS-MASS Collection, U.S. Army Military History Institute*; 1822 capitol building in Harrisburg. *Historical Society of Dauphin County.*

First published 2013

Manufactured in the United States

ISBN 978.1.62619.041.2

Library of Congress CIP data applied for.

Contents

Foreword

Pennsylvania earned its nickname as the "Keystone State" in the eighteenth century. Its geographic location among the thirteen British colonies along the Atlantic coast made it both physically and politically central to the new nation that declared independence in 1776. Its central role continued during and after the Revolutionary War and on into the politics and governance of the United States under the Articles of Confederation and the Constitution of 1787.

In the mid-nineteenth century, it remained key to preserving the United States when civil war threatened to tear the nation asunder. As the second-most populous state in the North, it furnished the second-largest number of troops to the Federal army. It had, moreover, horses to mount its twenty-two cavalry regiments, foodstuffs to provision its own soldiers (and many other blueclad units as well) and industry to supply the troops and support the war effort. Perhaps most significantly, it had coal: the energy source of the Industrial Revolution that fueled the Federal war effort. According to the census of 1860, 78 percent of all known coal deposits anywhere in the United States, north and south, were located in Pennsylvania. That state, moreover, contained 100 percent of known anthracite deposits, the clean-burning hard coal that powered the great steam frigates of the United States Navy.

Such war-making potentiality made Pennsylvania a bastion on the border between free states and slave states. From it, Federal forces could overawe wavering Maryland, encourage loyalist western Virginia and project power southward against the Confederate States of America. Pennsylvania, furthermore, proved a bulwark against invasion of the North. Some such invasions were only rumored, especially during the secession crisis and the first frantic months of civil war. Other potential incursions went unrealized, such as the Antietam Campaign in September 1862, the Jones-Imboden Raid in April 1863 and Morgan's Ohio Raid three months later. Three times, however, graycoats carried the war into the Keystone State: "Jeb" Stuart's second ride around McClellan in October 1862, John McCausland's burning of Chambersburg in July 1864 and the Great Invasion in the early summer of 1863 that culminated in the biggest battle of the war: Gettysburg.

The commonwealth's capital, Harrisburg, proved crucial to the war effort (1861–65). Troops were raised and mustered there, especially in the great Camp Curtin on the state fairgrounds just north of the city and also in other state camps in and around the city. The Regular Army even established its own Camp Greble there in 1861, the first regimental headquarters for the new 5th U.S. Artillery. Then, too, key east–west and north–south railroad lines intersected in Harrisburg. They brought troops from northern Pennsylvania and southern New York to the city and then hastened them to Hagerstown or Baltimore and onward to the fighting fronts. The great lateral trunk rail line from Philadelphia to Pittsburgh and on to the Midwest—so critical for shifting soldiers and supplies between Eastern and Western Theaters—crossed the Susquehanna River on the Rockville bridge just upstream from Harrisburg. The city, moreover, was not only a transportation hub but also a center for leadership: the seat of civil government throughout the Civil War and a major military headquarters from mid-June 1863 to late August 1864. All these factors underscored the city's importance to the Union war effort and made it a prime target for invading Confederates.

Many prominent persons lived in Harrisburg because of their civil or military duties, even though their permanent homes were elsewhere in the commonwealth or in the nation. For some major officials, however, Harrisburg *was* home, including Secretary of War Simon Cameron and Generals Joseph F. Knipe of the 46th Pennsylvania Infantry Regiment, Edward C. Williams of the 9th Pennsylvania Cavalry Regiment and George Zinn of the 84th Pennsylvania Infantry Regiment.

Yet Harrisburg was also home for people: ordinary citizens who experienced the excitement and encouragement, the apprehension and anxiety, the routine and regimen of war. Daily they went about their businesses and their lives, yet always they lived under the shadow of war.

Sometimes it was distant, where their husbands, fathers, brothers, sons, kinsfolk, friends and neighbors served at the front. Sometimes it was just across the river, as Butternut brigades brought the battlefield deep into Cumberland County, with Rockville and Harrisburg among their targets. Ever was it a reality that loomed over their lives.

These human emotions as well as military experiences are captured and conveyed in *Harrisburg and the Civil War: Defending the Keystone of the Union*, which covers Harrisburg throughout the war. The author, Mr. Cooper Wingert of Enola, Pennsylvania, is a remarkable young historian. He not only possesses passion for the Civil War but also has the productivity to share his interest with a broader readership. Although only fourteen years old, he has already written six other books on the Civil War. His dedication, diligence, productivity and persistence again bear fruit in his most important book to date. *Harrisburg and the Civil War* is a significant study of a significant city in the strains of Civil War. It makes an important contribution to understanding civilians at war. It belongs in every Civil War library.

Richard J. Sommers, PhD
Senior Historian
Army Heritage and Education Center
Army War College

Acknowledgements

Numerous persons have assisted me in the completion of this volume. Dr. Richard J. Sommers of the U.S. Army Military History Institute at Carlisle Barracks wrote the foreword to this volume, as well as advising me on various historical and research matters. Scott Mingus of York, Pennsylvania, helped to organize the table of contents and kindly reviewed the manuscript, offering his insight. Once again, John Heiser of Gettysburg constructed great maps to complement the text. Steve Bachmann and Ken Frew of the Historical Society of Dauphin County were also helpful in providing photographs and manuscripts from HSDC's extensive collections.

Chapter 1

Harrisburg's Initial Responses to the Civil War

All sorts of rumors were afloat, and the operators in the telegraph offices were besieged by anxious applicants.[1]
–Harrisburg Daily Patriot and Union, *April 15, 1861*

Since its founding in 1785 by John Harris Jr., Harrisburg, Pennsylvania, had seen unprecedented growth. In 1794, President George Washington passed through the region on his way to suppress the Whiskey Rebellion and was impressed by the bustling young town. After a brief stroll through the settlement, Washington opined that Harrisburg "is considerable for its age (of about eight or nine years)."[2] The growth continued long after Washington's eighteenth-century visit. In 1812, the state capital was relocated to Harrisburg. In the late 1830s, railroads made their appearance, and the sharp, ringing whistle of an incoming locomotive soon became a familiar sound to the residents.

It was not long before the emergent young town became an important railroad hub—various firms were soon competing to extend their lines to Harrisburg.[3] The Pennsylvania Railroad Company leased a small station built in 1837 by the Harrisburg and Lancaster Railroad. The thriving industry soon outgrew this small depot, and twenty years later—in 1857—a new and enlarged station was completed and again leased to the Pennsylvania Railroad. With a distinctive Italianate architectural style, the depot measured 400 feet in length by 103 feet in width. The structure additionally boasted "a dining saloon calculated to seat from two hundred and fifty to three

The first Pennsylvania Railroad depot, completed in 1837 and replaced in 1857. *Historical Society of Dauphin County.*

hundred persons; ladies' and gentlemen's reception rooms; water closets; and a number of offices, including one for the magnetic telegraph owned by the company." The building cost $58,000 and was first opened to rail traffic on August 1, 1857.[1]

The Philadelphia and Reading Railroad also had lines running into Harrisburg. The company had originally been established in 1833 with the goal in mind to complete a railroad extending from Reading to Philadelphia, which was completed six years later after some extended legal barriers. In 1853, the entrepreneurial rail line decided to expand westward, gaining control of the Lebanon Valley Railroad, a line running between Harrisburg and Reading. The Lebanon Valley had been chartered for that purpose—connecting Harrisburg and Reading—but had failed to reach Harrisburg. Although still referred to as the Lebanon Valley, the line was officially redesignated the Philadelphia and Reading Railroad, which was completed and first opened in January 1858. The Pennsylvania Railway entered Harrisburg from the south, while the Philadelphia and Reading curled in from the east—crossing the nearby Pennsylvania Canal by an "iron trestle bridge," with both railroads meeting a short distance above Market Street. There the railway continued northward as the Pennsylvania Railroad.

The Philadelphia and Reading depot was erected opposite the counterpart Pennsylvania Railroad station and between the latter junction of the two lines and the adjacent canal. "It was a homey, easy-going, ramshackle affair," later recalled one Harrisburger. "The canal bordered the eastern side and the

The second Pennsylvania Railroad depot, photographed in 1863. *Historical Society of Dauphin County.*

slow-moving canal boats, with the patient, plodding mules helped lend an air of sleepy drowsiness to the calm that enveloped the whole place." Compared to the Pennsylvania Railroad's Italianate 1857 station, the Philadelphia and Reading's depot appeared more like a low-set barn, considering the structure was only nineteen feet high. However, with three tracks running through it and more than forty windows, the building still contained "all the essentials of a first class depot."[5]

Seemingly always competing with Harrisburg's extensive railroad network was the Pennsylvania Canal, which ran through the city east of the capitol grounds and what later became the two railways. As New York developed the Erie Canal in the 1820s, the Pennsylvania legislature kept a watchful eye and authorized the construction of the "State Works" in 1826. Eventually, the line would stretch from Columbia northward to Harrisburg and from there would continue twelve miles northwest to the mouth of the Juniata River, where the main line continued west. At Hollidaysburg, the waterway temporarily ended and was linked to Johnstown to its west via the Allegheny Portage Railroad before continuing as a canal to Pittsburgh. The canal began operations in 1834 and would continue until 1901. In 1857, the state sold the majority of the State Works—including the canal running through the eastern part of Harrisburg—to the Pennsylvania Railroad company. By 1860, however, the canal was already in decline, largely due to the rapid growth of the railroad industry; by 1865, the State Works west of Hollidaysburg were no longer in operation.[6]

Arguably, Harrisburg is today best known for its many and extensive bridges spanning the Susquehanna River. During the mid-nineteenth century, the main way of passage into Harrisburg for foot traffic was the Camelback Bridge, completed in 1817. Named for its distinctive curvature, the privately owned toll bridge attracted much attention. What further separated the covered bridge from its counterparts was its interesting, barn-like design. When Charles Dickens crossed over the bridge, he found travel across the mile-long passage unbearable. Dickens detailed that because the bridge was "roofed and covered in on all sides," it

> was profoundly dark; perplexed, with great beams, crossing and recrossing it at every possible angle; and through the broad chinks and crevices in the floor, the rapid river gleamed, far down below, like a legion of eyes. We had no lamps; and as the horses stumbled and floundered through this place, towards the distant speck of dying light, it seemed interminable. I could not at first persuade myself as we rumbled heavily on, filling the bridge with hollow noises, and I held down my head to save it from the rafters above, but that I was in a painful dream; for I have often dreamed of toiling through such places, and as often argued, even at the time, "this cannot be reality."[7]

Unlike Dickens, Harrisburg citizens embraced their unique bridge. When speaking of the Camelback, city residents often cited several "distinguished visitors" who had crossed the river on it. Always being sure to mention Dickens, notwithstanding that the author had termed his journey across the Camelback a "painful dream," the Camelback was *their* bridge, and Dickens had mentioned *it*. The bridge itself had been built in two sections, known as the eastern section, extending from Forster's (later City) Island to Harrisburg, and the western section, linking Forster's Island with the western banks of the Susquehanna. The interior of the Camelback was divided into four separate compartments, two situated in the center for various vehicles, horses and livestock and the other two on each side for pedestrian traffic.[8]

In addition to the Camelback, Harrisburg and the surrounding vicinity was sprawling with railways and railroad bridges. Entering town from the east was the Philadelphia and Reading (Lebanon Valley) Railroad, which met the Pennsylvania Railroad, the latter arriving in Harrisburg from the south. The Pennsylvania Railroad continued north from Harrisburg and crossed to the Susquehanna's western bank by a bridge just south of Marysville—near where the Rockville bridge stands today. From there, the line extended northwest. The Northern Central Railway made its way down the eastern banks of the Susquehanna from the north but crossed the river on a bridge situated a short distance above the Pennsylvania Railroad bridge and Marysville, just below the small town of Dauphin. The Northern Central continued south along the Susquehanna's western bank. The Cumberland Valley Railroad, on the other hand, extended from Harrisburg, across the river on a bridge located alongside the Camelback, through Mechanicsburg, Carlisle, Shippensburg and—as its name implies—down the Cumberland Valley to Chambersburg.

Nestled near the center of the young town was an area referred to as Market Square. Beginning in the 1790s, "market days" were established, and farmers and grocers from Harrisburg and the surrounding vicinity gathered in the square, where they sold and bartered their goods. By 1807, "market sheds"—small, rectangular, pavilion-style structures—had made their appearance, and for the next eighty-odd years, they were among the familiar features of the city. Wednesdays and Saturdays were designated as market days in the square. In the northern section of Harrisburg, the continued expansion of the Fifth and Sixth Wards necessitated a market house be opened there. In 1860, the West Harrisburg Market House—later redesignated the Broad Street Market—debuted at the corner of Third and Verbeke Streets, with market days scheduled for Tuesdays and Fridays so that farmers could still attend the market in the square.[9]

By 1860, residents of Harrisburg could count more than a dozen hotels situated all about the city. Among the more prominent were the Brady House—which claimed "the advantage of being located nearest the Capitol"—Herr's Hotel, the European Hotel (also known as Brant's Hall), the State Capitol Hotel, the Pennsylvania House and the United States Hotel; situated on the square were two of the most visited, the Buehler House and the Jones House. A number of smaller inns also populated the city—Hoffman's, Mager's, the Park House, Bomgardner, Susquehanna, Franklin, Seven Stars "and a large number of others not in the heart of the city" all provided plenty of room to accommodate a large number of travelers.[10] The Brady House, operated by "Major" Brady, was situated in a five-story brick structure at the corner of Third and State Streets, adjacent to the capitol. "During the Civil War it was the scene of many stirring events and of many important political discussions." Located on the southern end of the capitol grounds was "Colonel" Omit's State Capitol Hotel, at the

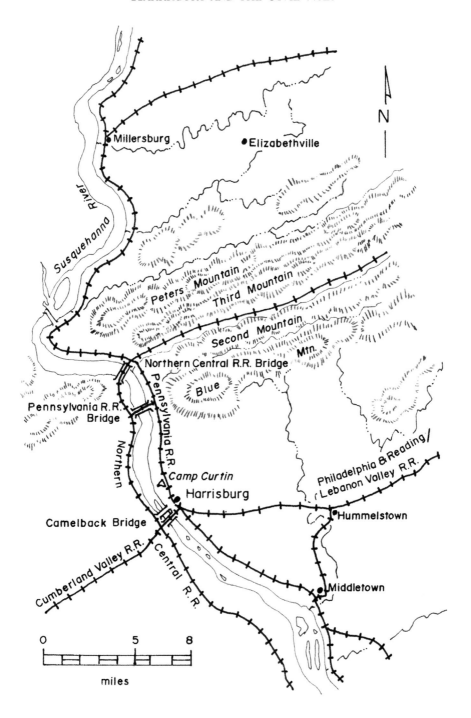

Railroads near Harrisburg, circa 1860. *Map by John Heiser.*

In 1853, a correspondent for the Boston journal *Gleason's Pictorial* traveled to the Pennsylvania Railroad bridge north of Harrisburg. The New Englander found the scenery north of the city "delightfully-attractive," noting that "the entire aspect of the neighborhood is wild and picturesque in its character…The scenery about this spot has all the softness of a splendid agricultural valley, teeming with spirited little villages, and imposing farm-houses, agreeably contrasting with the soft green aspect of bold and lofty mountain ranges, through which the river tamely and serenely winds its peaceful way, like a silver thread." The paper published the engraving here sketched from the Susquehanna's eastern banks. The bridge would figure prominently in the transportation of supplies and troops to and from Harrisburg during the war. *Author's collection.*

corner of Third and Walnut Streets. "During the sixties and seventies it was one of the most prominent hotels in the city, many of the leading political men of that day making it their headquarters."[11]

At the "extreme northeastern corner" of Market Square, near Strawberry Street, was the Buehler House, which traced its existence back to the early 1800s. After his disconcerting ride across the Camelback, Charles Dickens spent the night at the hotel, which he later praised in his *American Notes*. The English author described the establishment as a "snug hotel, which, though smaller and far less splendid than many we put up at, is raised above them all in my remembrance, by having for its landlord the most obliging, considerate, and gentlemanly person I ever had to deal with." The establishment was initially known as the Eagle Hotel because its sign showed "a beautiful spread eagle." In 1860, George J. Bolton took over as proprietor. That December, Bolton opened a restaurant "under" the Buehler house. "The rooms have been papered, painted, and fitted up with gas fixtures, so as to give everything a cheerful look, and we are told that the *cuisine* will be under the immediate supervision of an eminent professor of the art of cooking," reported the *Patriot*. "The intention of the proprietor is to serve up all kinds of game in season, to be had in the Eastern or Western markets, and particular attention is to be paid to the oyster and ale departments." Apparently, William Buehler—the structure's namesake—retained some form of ownership over the establishment, and Bolton assumed the role of landlord. The *Patriot* later commented, "Mr. [William] Buehler, the owner of the premises, has displayed a spirit of commendable liberality in refitting and refurnishing this favorite first class establishment from cellar to garret, and we feel certain that Mr. Bolton will make a popular landlord." During the Civil War, the structure was still known as the Buehler House.[12] In September 1866, President Andrew Johnson visited the hotel, accompanied by General Ulysses S. Grant and Admiral David G. Farragut.[13]

In the late eighteenth century, a "small frame building" was erected on the southeastern corner of what came to be known as Market Square. The structure was dubbed the "Washington Inn" or the "Washington House"—the insignificant inn's claim to fame being the 1794 visit of President George Washington while he was en route to quell the Whiskey Rebellion. In 1853, the hotel was razed, rebuilt and christened the Jones House after its architect. Prominent guests soon became a recurrent theme at the hotel. In October 1860, the Jones House played host to Albert Edward, Prince of Wales. After somehow managing to escape a thronging crowd surrounding his quarters at the Jones House, the prince and his entourage drove in open carriages to the capitol and ascended the dome to a wondrous view. "There you see the silent Susquehanna, coiled like a serpent in a garden, and spotted with flowery islets," noted one of the royal following. "You have that pleasant antithesis afforded by an intermingling of hill and valley, mirror-like glimpses of water, verdure, forest, and a town with eleven thousand inhabitants, and after the survey of the prospect you return to terra firma, feeling well repaid for the trouble incurred in ascending the steps." By 1860, the Jones House was under the proprietorship of "Colonel" Wells Coverly, who was reportedly "making arrangements to increase his accommodations" during the winter of 1860.[14]

This postwar photograph (circa 1876–89) depicts a typical market day at Harrisburg's Market Square. Visible in the foreground are the market sheds, and near the center of the photograph are the horse car tracks of the Harrisburg City Passenger Railway, which debuted in 1865. In the right background, note the Buehler House, known as the Bolton House at the time of this image. *Historical Society of Dauphin County.*

Perhaps the Jones House's most famous guest arrived shortly before the war broke out in April 1861. En route to his inauguration in Washington in February 1861, President-elect Abraham Lincoln and family were quartered at the hotel. Arriving in Harrisburg around noon on February 22, Lincoln had been informed while in Philadelphia the previous evening that if he were to continue to Washington as planned—meaning a trip through the pro-Southern city of Baltimore—it would only be with "grave peril to his life." After dining at the Jones House that evening, Lincoln was secreted out of the city and arrived safely in Washington.[15]

The picturesque capitol grounds were another of Harrisburg's highlights in the mid-nineteenth century. A glimpse of the surrounding country from the dome captivated visitors and, during the 1860s, soldiers passing through the city. Immediately south of the capitol was the state arsenal, where many of the arms used by Pennsylvania soldiers during the war were stored.

Located at the intersection of Market Street and Raspberry Alley (later redesignated Court Street) was the county courthouse. To meet the needs of the growing city, a new courthouse was constructed during the spring and summer of 1860 and was in operation by the fall of 1860. In the rear of the courthouse, facing Walnut Street, was the Gothic-style county prison.

Advertisement for the Jones House, circa 1860. *Historical Society of Dauphin County.*

This prison—which stood throughout the war—was completed in 1841. Constructed of "fine light granite from Chester or Montgomery country," the prison was two stories high and crowned by an octagonal tower. The structure fronting Walnut Street was reserved for the residence and office of the prison keeper, and in the rear of this building was the actual prison, the two connected by a ten-foot-wide corridor. The prison itself was described as "a plain limestone building, two stories high, containing forty cells, each fifteen feet in length and seven and a half in width." Supplying water to the city was the Harrisburg Water Works. The water house was located along the banks of the Susquehanna at the western end of North Street. There the water was pumped into the reservoir, the latter situated on high ground immediately north of the capitol. On the other hand, Harrisburg's Gas Works consisted of two "handsome brick structures," located near the Pennsylvania Railroad, which supplied gas to the city's residents through twenty-eight thousand feet of pipe, as well as an additional mile and a half of pipe reaching to the State Lunatic Hospital northeast of the city.[16]

During the mid-nineteenth century, Harrisburg experienced a massive population increase, accompanied by a growing trend of industrialization. In 1850, the population of Harrisburg was 7,834. Just ten years later, in 1860, Harrisburg boasted a populace of 13,405, nearly double what it had been in 1850, and was now large enough to be chartered a city.[17] Not only had its population skyrocketed, but by 1860, Harrisburg was also home to an impressive array of businesses and industries. Situated along the banks of the Susquehanna on the city's northern limits was the Harrisburg Cotton Manufacturing Company, commonly known as the Cotton Mill or Cotton Factory, constructed in 1849. Four years later, in 1853, William O. Hickok founded the Eagle Works on a plot of land north of the railroad depot and alongside the Pennsylvania Railroad tracks. A bookbinder by trade, Hickok's Harrisburg bindery burned to the ground in 1844. After this tragic twist, Hickok opened a small store featuring bookbinding specialties on Market Street. Among his most famous tinkerings was his "Improved Ruling Machine," designed to mechanically line writing paper. The products his Eagle Works turned out were not far off from Hickok's former practice. The plant produced various presses, cutting machines, ink, desks and an assemblage of other crafty products. Among his bestsellers was his famous portable cider press, which he retailed for $35. However, unpaid debt amounting to $30,000 plagued Hickok, whose property was sold at a sheriff's sale in 1856 to prominent Harrisburger James McCormick. Hickok's Eagle Works remained operational, with Hickok himself continuing under the name of publisher Isaac G. McKinney & Company. Throughout the course of the war, however, Hickok would redeem his name. The bookbinder reportedly worked as an agent for James McCormick, who had purchased the works; Hickok settled his debts, and became president of the city council.

By 1860, Harrisburg also had flourishing iron and steel production. In 1840, the firm Hunt & Son launched Harrisburg's first significant rolling mill at the intersection of Second and Paxton Streets, alongside the canal. The plant was not long-lived, destroyed by fire shortly after its founding. However, five years later, in 1845, Pratt & Son—headed by Jared Pratt of Baltimore—erected a new rolling mill on the Hunt & Son ruins. Situated just north of Hickok's Eagle Works was the Central Iron Works, more often called the "Hot Pot" or Bailey's Rolling Mill. Brothers Charles and George Bailey established the facility along Herr Street, above the capitol and near the railroad and canal in 1853. The city also boasted two furnaces. The "Porter Furnace," originated by former governor David Porter in 1850, was Harrisburg's first anthracite furnace. Situated on the opposite (east) side of the canal from Hickok's Eagle Works, Porter was found insolvent in 1858, and the furnace was sold to Absalom Price and William Hancock by the Harrisburg Bank in 1860. Two Lancaster entrepreneurs—George Bryan and David Longenecker—founded the Keystone Furnace south of the city in 1853. The Keystone (also known as the Paxton Furnace) became Harrisburg's second anthracite furnace.

Another prominent industry in Harrisburg during the mid-nineteenth century was the Harrisburg Car Manufacturing Company, also known as the Harrisburg Car Factory. Profiting from Harrisburg's growing dependence on the railroad industry, the Car Factory was established in 1854 above the capitol and alongside the canal. The business produced rolling stock for the railroad through the 1860s until flames engulfed the plant in 1872, whereupon a new—and not to mention significantly larger—plant was constructed.[18] The city was also home to the State Hospital for the Insane—christened in a rather insensitive manner the State Lunatic Hospital and often called the "lunatic asylum"—completed in 1851. The brainchild of mental-rights activist Dorothea Dix, the building—located east of the Pennsylvania Railroad and Canal (near the present intersection of Cameron and Maclay Streets)—served as a curiosity to soldiers stationed near the city during the war, some of whom took time to visit the facility.[19]

Throughout the 1860s, Harrisburg had two main newspapers. However, in the antebellum years, residents were overwhelmed with numerous competing journals. Considering that Harrisburg was a predominantly Democratic audience, papers that leaned Democratic in their politics were plentiful—more than five Democratic journals were in publication in the years leading up to the war: the *Oracle*, the *Democratic State Journal*, the *Keystone*, the *Democratic Union* and the *Patriot*. In 1858, several of these publications merged to form the *Patriot and Union*. Although the Democratic papers had the upper hand in political leanings, the Republican *Telegraph* enjoyed its role as Harrisburg's leading newspaper throughout the nineteenth-century. Founded in 1831 by Theophilus Fenn to promote ideals of the Whig Party—a forerunner of the Republican Party—the paper was transformed into the city's Republican journal during the 1850s, in large part through the influence of its new proprietor, George Bergner, and other behind-the-scenes maneuvering characteristic of part-time Harrisburg resident-politician Simon Cameron. In 1855, the *Telegraph* was purchased by Bergner, a staunch Republican and German immigrant who came to America at age twelve. Bergner was no stranger to newspapers, having originally arrived in Harrisburg in 1834 as the publisher of several German newspapers. Beginning in 1857, he published the *Legislative Record* in addition to the *Telegraph*. The German immigrant's political influence only strengthened with the election of Abraham Lincoln, who appointed him postmaster of Harrisburg, an office that he held through 1866. The *Patriot* and *Telegraph* soon emerged as combative rivals, frequently taking jabs at each other.[20] When news of the war first reached Harrisburg, the *Telegraph* suggested that its rival journal display the Palmetto flag—the state

Postwar photograph of the Jones House, with the market sheds visible in the foreground, circa 1887–89. *Historical Society of Dauphin County.*

banner of South Carolina, where the war's first shots were fired—opining that the *Patriot* editorial staff "must be the only people in Harrisburg who can possibly be gratified with the news from Charleston."[21]

Harrisburg's unrelenting industrial and economic growth came to a screeching halt on Friday, April 12, 1861, when Southern forces opened fire on a Union garrison at Fort Sumter, located in Charleston Harbor. Word of this engagement—the opening hostilities of the war—reached Harrisburg the following day as the action near Charleston carried on. Immediately, citizens of Harrisburg had strong reactions. "The war has thus been begun by the Secessionists, and on them rests the responsibility," declared the *Telegraph.*[22] "The excitement in this city on Saturday morning, on account of the startling news from the South, was intense," noted the editors of the *Patriot.* "All sorts of rumors were afloat, and the operators in the telegraph offices were besieged by anxious applicants to ascertain if the intelligence was correct. Knots of persons were congregated at the street corners discussing the news, and everybody appeared to be in fever heat to get the particulars." When papers from Philadelphia and New York arrived in the city around noon, "the demand for them was so great that the supply was immediately exhausted."[23]

As the sun rose on the morning of Sunday, April 14, the overall excitement in the city was unabated. In the opinion of the *Patriot*, the fervor "had rather increased." "Rumors of all kinds were in circulation, purporting to have come from Charleston—the truth or falsity of which seemed to exercise the mind of the people," the Democratic paper continued. "We are informed that the preachers in most of our churches referred to the exciting state of affairs in their pulpits yesterday, and fervent prayers were offered to the Throne of Grave for the preservation of our country."[24] The following day—April 15, one day after the Federal garrison at Fort Sumter surrendered—President Abraham Lincoln called for seventy-five thousand volunteers to suppress the rebellion.[25] A markedly increased seriousness immediately spread over Harrisburg upon word of Lincoln's call. That evening, a meeting was held at the "Exchange"—the Masonic Hall on Walnut Street between Third and Raspberry Alley (later Court Street)—which was decorated with "large and small American Flags" for the occasion. Harrisburg lawyer "Colonel" A.J. Herr delivered a "patriotic address" explaining the causes of the war and concluded his remarks by encouraging young men to rally in defense of the Union. The following evening, "one of the largest assemblages every convened in this city" gathered at the courthouse, where Herr and others addressed the immense crowd.[26]

Harrisburg was not alone in its increased patriotic ardor. Throughout the Keystone State, many Pennsylvanians eagerly flocked to Philadelphia, Pittsburgh and Harrisburg to enlist. For twenty-eight-year-old Isaac Rothermel Dunkelberger, a resident of Sunbury, Pennsylvania, the surrender of Fort Sumter "had the effect of an electric shock…All doubt had been dispelled by this overt act, all hope of a peaceable solution was abandoned. The farmer stopped his plow, the mechanic dropped his tools, the merchant closed his doors, and professional men closed their offices."[27]

When Dunkelberger arrived in Harrisburg around 10:00 a.m. on April 18, he found a city buzzing with excitement and military prestige.[28] The "Cameron Guards," a prewar Harrisburg militia unit dating back to the Mexican-American War, was parading through the city as it attempted to entice the men of Harrisburg to enlist and fill up its ranks. The company was captained by Jacob M. Eyster, a Gettysburg native and the son of General Jacob Eyster, who commanded Adams and York County troops in the War of 1812. Born in 1816, Eyster was educated at the Harrisburg Academy, and at age eighteen he was part of a surveying party for the stretch of the Pennsylvania Canal between Harrisburg and Lewistown. After his dabble in surveying, Eyster returned to Harrisburg, where he apprenticed the trade of tinning and afterward entered an engineering course at Pennsylvania (later Gettysburg) College in his native town. Eyster participated in several other surveys—notably that of the Pennsylvania Railroad from Harrisburg to Columbia—before settling down to a teaching position at the Lancastrian school on East Walnut Street in Harrisburg. While there, he formed a company out of his scholars, christened the "Junior Guard." "He was so proud of them that he visited Lancaster and Philadelphia in 1845 and '46 and met with a great reception." In 1852, fellow Harrisburg resident General Edward C. Williams named him deputy sheriff, and Eyster was subsequently elected sheriff in 1858. And on April 18, 1861, Eyster was captain of the Cameron Guards as they paraded throughout his adopted home town, trying to enlist new recruits. The Guards' attempt at enticement worked, subduing not only other Harrisburgers but Dunkelberger as well. "Here was my chance," reminisced the Sunbury resident. "I promptly signed the roll, although I did not know a man in the Company."[29]

The Cameron Guards included, by the beginning of May 1861, four companies that had been raised in Harrisburg, with others still organizing.

Sergeant Isaac R. Dunkelberger.
U.S. Army Military History Institute.

The State Capital Guard was organized by Harrisburg newspaper editor William B. Sipes. At the outbreak of the war, Sipes was the editor and proprietor of the *State Sentinel*. Eager to do his part in the coming conflict, he sold the *Sentinel* to the editors of the *Patriot and Union*, who discontinued the paper. Sipes, at age thirty, soon went about forming the State Capital Guard, which was mustered in on April 20 and was eventually designated Company I, 2nd Pennsylvania.[30] The "Lochiel Greys" and the "Verbeke Rifles" were also formed in late April 1861 and remained in Harrisburg throughout early May before departing the city. The Lochiel Greys, captained by thirty-year-old Henry McCormick of Harrisburg, were later incorporated as Company F, 25th Pennsylvania, while the Verbeke Rifles, under fifty-four-year-old Captain John Nevin, became Company E, 15th Pennsylvania.[31] Eyster's Cameron Guards would be designated Company E, 1st Pennsylvania. On the evening of April 20, the city's two earliest-organized companies—the Cameron Guards and the State Capital Guard—departed the city. "Harrisburg has witnessed many a day of rejoicing and festivity," opined the *Telegraph*, "but never before has she witnessed such a scene as that of Saturday last in the departure of the Guards."[32]

Harrisburg's many businesses and factories did not shy away from declaring their patriotic sentiments during the war's opening days. At Bailey's Rolling Mill on Herr Street, "a large and magnificent flag of the Stars and Stripes has been flung to the breeze." Similar displays were made by a number of other businesses within the city. The Harrisburg Car Factory, Porter's Furnace (then in the hands of Absalom Price and William Hancock and often referred to as Price and Hancock's furnace) and Hickok's Eagle Works all unfurled "magnificent" banners. Even the typically gloomy county prison bore a flag raised over its turret, "giving that usually somber-looking structure quite a cheerful appearance." But perhaps no establishment in Harrisburg displayed its patriotic ardor as much as the Jones House; proprietor Wells Coverly made sure that each and every one of the structure's one-hundred-plus windows was adorned with the Stars and Stripes, while also flying two large flags from the rooftop and another over the main entrance.

In the meantime, "[n]early all the ladies" of Harrisburg put themselves to work sewing haversacks for the soldiers. "Several thousands were made at the cotton mill alone," reported the *Patriot*, "where a large number of sewing machines were at work." A few days later, the *Patriot* advised Harrisburg's patriotic women to "now turn their attention to supplying the surgeons of the different regiments with lint and bandages. The former can be manufactured in every family where old pieces of linen can be found." Even a full month later, the patriotic zeal had still not faded. A group of women from Harrisburg raised money for "two or three webs of muslin, which they intend making up into shirts" for those soldiers passing through the city who presented a "ragged condition."[33]

Across the commonwealth, the male population had been mobilized, forming companies galore. As many of these eager volunteers arrived in Harrisburg, there was no place designated to receive them, and the soldiers-to-be quickly piled up at the railroad depot or other locations around town. When volunteer Calvin Pardee's company arrived in Harrisburg on the evening of April 18, he and his war-bound comrades were forced to sleep on the floor of the capitol. "[T]here is but little discipline," detailed Pardee. Other companies also entered the capitol, typically creating a disorderly upheaval throughout the structure. "Another company of volunteers supposed to be a company from Allentown has just entered this building and there is more of an uproar than ever and it is now utterly impossible to write," he penned to his father late that evening.[34] Pardee was not alone in his experience. Many volunteers found themselves crammed in the city's churches and taverns, setting up camp on the lawn of the capitol or, like Pardee, within the structure itself. When the "Standing Stone Guards" of Huntingdon arrived in Harrisburg in the predawn hours of April 21, the men were accommodated at the Buehler House. "There being no beds empty," reported Sergeant William H. Fleuner, "we were compelled to sleep on chairs, floors, etc. or else not sleep at all." After breakfast, a number of the Huntingdon boys paid a visit to the capitol, which they found "completely filled with 'soger b'hoys' and citizens."[35]

It was painfully obvious to state and city officials that a place of rendezvous needed to be established in order to receive the overwhelming number of soldiers pouring into the city. A dysfunctional trend had set in—upon their arrival, companies were crammed into various structures about Harrisburg, where they remained with nowhere to go. Among those early arrivals who were quartered in various city buildings were the "First Defenders." These five companies—eventually part of the 25th Pennsylvania Infantry—gained their famous title for being the first Union troops to arrive for the defense of Washington, D.C. All five companies of the soon-to-be-crowned First Defenders passed through Harrisburg on their way to the nation's capital and were mustered in at the Keystone State capital. Private Curtis C. Pollock, a First Defender from the Washington Artillery—later Company H, 25th Pennsylvania—left a detailed account of his company's arrival and forgettable experience in Harrisburg. On April 17, Pollock and his comrades started from

Pottsville, reaching Harrisburg at about 8:30 p.m. that evening. Upon their arrival, the men of the Washington Artillery were "conducted to our quarters over a Lager beer Saloon," where the company spent the night. For Pollock, the disagreeable part of his stay in Harrisburg began with supper, which was served at the saloon: "[W]e had our supper in the Saloon and had beans and pork with bread and butter and coffee without any sugar or milk…it was the dirtiest place I have been in for a long time. After a person was done they took the plate and threw what was on it on the floor and then wiped the plate with a dirty towel." The company drilled late into the night and then laid down to sleep as best they could. "[W]e had to sleep on the floor and on straw," reported Pollock. "[A] parcel of us went out to a livery stable and brought twenty four bundles which was scattered around the floor." Much to Pollock's displeasure, his company breakfasted at the saloon the following morning before it was hustled to the railroad depot, where Captain Seneca G. Simmons—a Harrisburg resident and Regular Army officer—mustered him and the rest of the First Defenders into service at dawn. The First Defenders were then transported to Baltimore via the Northern Central Railway and from there to Washington.[36]

Governor Andrew Gregg Curtin was not oblivious to the fact that a place of rendezvous was needed somewhere near the city. On April 18, Curtin directed Harrisburg resident and prewar militiaman General Edward C. Williams to establish a camp to facilitate the mustering, training and other needs of these incoming volunteers on the Dauphin County Agricultural Fairgrounds north of the city. It was Curtin's intention to christen the site Camp Union.[37] Born on February 10, 1820, Edward Charles Williams was by 1860 a well-known and respected citizen of Harrisburg. Educated in the public schools of Philadelphia, Williams apprenticed as a bookbinder and later established the firm Clyde & Williams, bookbinders and stationers, in Harrisburg. The firm performed binding services for the state. Shortly after his arrival in Harrisburg, Williams began his military career when he joined the "old Dauphin Guards," a long-established military company in Harrisburg. Williams saw service with the Dauphin Guards when the company was called to suppress an 1844 riot in his native Philadelphia. In December 1846, Williams responded to calls for volunteers to serve in the Mexican-American War by raising a company from the streets of his adopted hometown that he christened the "Cameron Guards." The determined Harrisburg resident pushed his company so hard that it completed an arduous, 150-mile trek from Chambersburg to Pittsburgh through fifteen inches of snow in four days. Williams's Harrisburg Company formed part of the 2nd Pennsylvania

Brigadier General Edward C. Williams. After serving as a brigadier general of Pennsylvania volunteers for three months, Williams obtained the colonelcy of the 9th Pennsylvania Cavalry in October 1861; he resigned one year later. *Historical Society of Dauphin County.*

Regiment. Upon his return from Mexico, Captain Williams was elected sheriff of Dauphin County in 1850, running as an Independent.[38]

During the decade before the war broke out in 1861, Williams remained active in the Pennsylvania militia. In February 1854, he became captain of the "National Guards," another prewar Dauphin County militia company.

Williams was elected brigadier general of the 3rd Brigade, 5th Division of Pennsylvania militia on June 6, 1859. This brigade was primarily composed of Harrisburg-area militia. By 1861, General Williams was a prominent citizen of Harrisburg, and he was someone Curtin could rely on to establish Camp Union.[39]

Accompanying Williams on April 18 was his evidently close friend, fellow Harrisburger and aide-de-camp, Joseph Farmer Knipe. Born in Mount Joy, Lancaster County, on March 30, 1823, Knipe was the fourth of ten children of Henry and Elizabeth Knipe. After a standard education in the schools of Manheim and Lebanon, Knipe journeyed to Philadelphia, where it was intended that he would apprentice the trade of a shoemaker, like his older brother. Apparently Knipe had little enthusiasm for the craft, and in April 1842, the Lancaster County native enlisted for five years in Company I, 2nd Artillery. At the time of his enlistment, Knipe had recently turned nineteen—however, he reported his age as twenty-one, most likely because he did not have his parents' consent. During Dorr's Rebellion in Rhode Island, Knipe served in a reinforcing detachment sent as a precautionary measure by the Federal government. After fighting in the Mexican-American War, Knipe returned to civilian life. He arrived

Major Joseph F. Knipe. In August 1861, Knipe was commissioned colonel of the 46th Pennsylvania Infantry and was wounded at the Battle of Cedar Mountain one year later. In April 1863, he was promoted a brigadier general of volunteers, and while home that same summer, still suffering from his Cedar Mountain wounds, he led a brigade of New York National Guard troops to defend Harrisburg. After the war, Knipe served as postmaster of Harrisburg and died in the city in 1901. *MOLLUS-MASS Collection, U.S. Army Military History Institute.*

in Harrisburg in October 1848 as an employee of the Pennsylvania Railroad, part of the company's mail-handling service. By the outbreak of the war, Knipe was the rail line's Harrisburg mail agent. In May 1851, he married Elizabeth Sarah Hagan of Carlisle, with whom he would eventually father twelve children, six before the war. Knipe accepted an appointment as aide-de-camp from his apparently good friend, General Edward Williams, on June 10, 1859—only four days after Williams had been elected brigadier general of militia.[40]

Since 1857, a tract of ground situated roughly one mile north of the city had been used as the Dauphin County Agricultural Fairgrounds. "The spot selected was that above what is now Maclay street," reported one early Harrisburg historian, "fifty acres of almost perfectly level land, extending along Maclay street from what is now Seventh to Fifth, and on the north to Reel's lane, above what is now Schuylkill street." The gate to the fairgrounds was located near Ridge Road, a dusty lane leading northward to the site from the city limits. The dusty thoroughfare was so named for the ridge that once extended north from the capitol grounds "for some distance" as an extension of Capitol Hill. Encircling the fairgrounds was a towering sixteen-foot board fence. "A row of sheds along [modern] Fifth street to Reel's lane was used for storing hay and feed for the stock on exhibition; the cattle, horses, pigs, and chickens themselves were made at home in stalls along the Seventh street side of the fair grounds." Situated near the center of the grounds was Floral Hall, also known as the Park House. During the days of the Dauphin County Agricultural Fair, Floral Hall "housed the machinery, [and] horticultural and domestic arts exhibits."[41] The last fair held on the grounds, in September 1860, fell short of expectations. The *Telegraph* reported:

> *The County Fair opened this morning, under somewhat discouraging auspices. We were on the ground at eleven o'clock, at which time the cattle stalls, the poultry cages, and the tent devoted to vegetables were comparatively empty. Floral Hall is filling up gradually, but the display in that department will fall short of what is has been at former Fairs. The number and variety of agricultural implements on exhibition will not be equal to that of last year. But very few people are in attendance from the rural districts; and all indications to-day are that the Fair will prove at least a partial failure. Many of our mechanics, and other citizens, who went to a great deal of trouble and expense last year in decorating Floral Hall, have contributed nothing this season. Not more than fifty head of*

cattle are on exhibition thus far; and there is but one solitary contributor to the vegetable department in the big tent.[12]

However, on April 18, 1861, the fairgrounds were about to breathe new life as Williams, Knipe and an assemblage of soldiers trekked northward from Harrisburg. Following closely behind were Knipe's wife and two daughters. "We had a fine time watching the soldiers who were busy getting the camp into shape and who kept coming through the gates continually," later recalled Knipe's daughter, Teresa. The three women watched from their "big open carriage" as Knipe led a group of soldiers toward Floral Hall. "He climbed a ladder and came out on the roof with a flag in his hand," Teresa continued. "When he had it attached to the ropes he shouted: 'What shall we name this camp? I propose the name of Governor Curtin.'" Although under orders from Governor Curtin to name the site Camp Union, Knipe, Williams and Harrisburg resident Captain Seneca Simmons determined to christen it in honor of the governor. Teresa watched as the "soldiers all cheered and so did every one else." Her father, meanwhile, "stood on the roof and waved his hat." He then ran the banner up the mast, and the first flag was raised over Camp Curtin.[13]

Williams quickly took temporary charge of Camp Curtin. On the afternoon of April 18—after Knipe hoisted the flag over Floral Hall—an estimated two hundred tents were placed on the fairgrounds. By the following afternoon, a staggering twenty-nine companies occupied the camp. Within a day, Camp Curtin began functioning as the troop facilitation center it had been established to be. A number of companies entered the encampment on the morning of April 19. "The commissary department, during the day, supplied all the wants of the men," reported the *Patriot*. "Those of them unarmed will remain here until they are furnished by the General Government with arms and equipments." The "four or five" companies that were armed and uniformed left Harrisburg the following morning after spending the night in Camp Curtin.[14] Thirty-two companies were sworn in on April 20 alone. During the period from April 18 to April 22, a reported seventy-four companies—totaling 5,467 men—were mustered in at Camp Curtin.[15]

In the afternoon hours of April 20, many in Camp Curtin witnessed what they believed was a good omen for the coming conflict. "[T]he day was warm and beautiful, and our camp was literally packed with soldiers," penned Corporal Sidney T. Muffley of the "Curtin Guards" of Bellefonte, one of the many companies massed within the camp. A "number of persons" had scaled Floral Hall and were prepared to run the Stars and Stripes up the mast. "The bunting was raised to about half-mast," continued Muffley, "when an Eagle was discovered high in the air, soaring toward our camp from the South, as if to ask our protection from the blood-stained murderers of our happy Union; the noble freedom loving eagle when over the emblem of our country, soared in a circle over it, each time coming nearer the flag, seemed for a moment when directly over it, to remain motionless, then majestically rising it slowly soaring [*sic*] away to the North." Isaac Dunkelberger, the Sunbury resident who had joined the Cameron Guards, recalled that the eagle "made several circumferences during the most intense cheering I ever heard." As the bird continued "winding its way over our camp," the soldiers in attendance "rushed to the upper end of the ground greeting it with cheer after cheer." The bird continued in a southwesterly direction and was watched intently by the fervent crowd as it disappeared into the distance. "So enthusiastic were the soldiers," Muffley explained, "that every man gave vent to his patriotic feelings, so thrilling was the scene that had it been witnessed by the traitors they would have been filled with feelings of remorse and shame at the absurd attempt they have made to destroy the blessings of the land of their birth." "It may have been an accident," reflected Dunkelberger, "but it made a profound impression on many of those who saw it. It was looked upon as a favorable omen—an inspiration for hope."[46]

Among a number of officers instrumental in Camp Curtin's first days was Major General William High Keim. The son of Benneville and Mary (High) Keim (the daughter of General William High), Keim was born on June 13, 1813, in Reading. At age twelve, he entered the Military Academy at Mount Airy, near Philadelphia, from which he graduated in 1829. After his graduation, Keim returned home and joined his father's business, at the time "one of the largest general hardware stores" in Reading. Keim never lost interest in the military, however, and he soon entered the state militia. "His early military training gave him a natural taste for military affairs and he found much gratification in the volunteer service of the State militia." Before he turned seventeen, Keim had reached the rank of orderly sergeant in the "Washington Grays," and in 1837, the Reading native succeeded his cousin as captain of the outfit. Rapid promotion continued through 1842, when Keim was elected major general and given command of the 5th Division of Pennsylvania militia. The 5th Division was composed of militia units from Berks, Lebanon, Dauphin and Schuylkill

Brigadier General William H. Keim. *MOLLUS-MASS Collection, U.S. Army Military History Institute.*

Counties. General Edward Williams commanded the 3rd Brigade of Keim's 5th Division, the former consisting almost entirely of militia from Harrisburg and the surrounding vicinity.

In 1848, Keim was elected the second mayor of Reading. After serving as mayor, he was voted to Congress in November 1858 during a special election to fill a seat opened by the resignation of J. Glancy Jones. Keim served less than three months, his short term expiring in March 1859. Later that same year, he was elected surveyor general of Pennsylvania. In 1860, the Reading native suggested to newly elected governor Andrew Curtin that "the Commonwealth should be put in a condition of defense, inasmuch as the signs of political discontent over the election of Lincoln indicated civil strife." When the war finally arrived in April 1861, Keim reported to Harrisburg and offered his services to Governor Curtin, who appointed him a major general of Pennsylvania volunteers on April 20. Two days later, on the morning of April 22, Keim was in the second story of Floral Hall—which had been appropriated as the headquarters building for Camp

Lieutenant Colonel Washington H.R. Hangen, the first commandant of Camp Curtin. *MOLLUS-MASS Collection, U.S. Army Military History Institute.*

Curtin—"busily engaged" in his duties. At Camp Curtin, Keim played a critical role in the organization of Pennsylvania's three-month regiments. During the summer of 1861, he served as second-in-command to Major General Robert Patterson, a fellow prewar militiaman, in the first of many abortive campaigns in the Shenandoah Valley. Mustered out on July 21, his ties to Harrisburg did not end then. Keim was made a brigadier general in the United States volunteer service on December 20, 1861, for which he resigned from his position as Pennsylvania's surveyor general.[47]

By May 1862, the Reading native was on the Virginia Peninsula with the Army of the Potomac. At the Battle of Williamsburg on May 5, 1862, Keim, although "too sick to be on duty," mounted a horse, departed the hospital and led his brigade into battle. "Though under fire nearly the whole time, he was perfectly calm." A Southern shell exploded "almost under" his horse, causing all around him to turn "pale with fear" and covering the fearless general with mud. After the battle had concluded, army commander George McClellan personally complimented Keim. However, three days later, Keim found extreme difficulty when writing a report of the engagement—he explained that his report was "imperfect…owing to sever indisposition." Keim reluctantly requested a furlough to return home to Harrisburg, where his family had taken up temporary residence. Never able to recover, he died in Harrisburg on May 18, 1862.[48]

Another influential figure in Camp Curtin's first days was Lieutenant Colonel Washington H.R. Hangen of the 9th Pennsylvania Infantry, who served as the camp's first commandant in late April and early May 1861 after Williams's departure.[49] One major problem Hangen, Keim, Knipe, Simmons and all those involved in Camp Curtin's first days encountered was that of food shortages. Thousands of volunteers were constantly arriving, and large quantities of rations were necessary to feed them. Early on in Camp Curtin's existence, the government gave contracts to civilian butchers and bakers. Harrisburger Alex Kosure was charged with furnishing meat for the camp. Brothers Charles and Harry Roumfort secured the main contract for supplying bread. Subcontracts were issued to other bakers, among them Thomas Findley and William Miller. These civilian bakers continued to supply Camp Curtin with bread until the government completed its own bakery near the corner of Fourth and Chestnut Streets during the summer of 1863. "The ovens never became cold, as they were run day and night by a double set of bakers," recalled Harrisburg resident Francis Hoy. The bakery's proximity to the railroad depot—where the "Soldiers' Retreat" or "Soldiers' Rest" was located, "not twenty rods away"—also made it ideal to furnish warm bread to the soldiers quartered there.[50] The "immense cullinary [sic] resources" of the nearby State Lunatic Hospital were additionally "placed at the disposal of the Government" almost immediately after Camp Curtin's establishment.[51]

Perhaps Harrisburg's most patriotic act during the war came from residents John B. Simon and Eby Byers. Out of the goodness of their hearts, the two Harrisburgers established the "Soldiers' Rest" or "Soldiers' Retreat" to care for sick and wounded soldiers passing through the city. Simon and Byers kept the establishment running with funds from their own pockets, as well as "voluntary aid" from their fellow citizens. Ideally located beside the Pennsylvania Railroad depot, the structure also fed incoming and outgoing soldiers in addition to housing and caring for those who were sick.[52] Reporters from the *Telegraph* visited the rest in August 1864 and later detailed:

> *This neat little Rest is handsomely furnished. The floor is nearly carpeted, and the beds are clean and comfortable[.] Nothing is wanted to render the*

place attractive, and a fit receptacle for the brave soldiers who have been smitten by disease. Among the decorations we notice the stars and stripes, the dear old flag upon which our patriotic defenders love to gaze. The patients are attended by ladies—those ministering angels—whose attentions are calculated to alleviate the sufferings of the sick. No doubt the Rest will be remembered by those brave men long after they return to the field of strife. It is well enough to repeat here what we have already recorded in these columns, that our good friend, Eby Byers, Esq., overlooks the sources necessary to the maintenance of the Rest with a vigi[l]ance which constantly keeps them flowing in abundance.[53]

Just as the editors of the *Telegraph* predicted, at least one soldier had a distinctive recollection of the rest. Edgar A. Walters of the 195[th] Pennsylvania, who had missed his regiment's departure from Harrisburg, enjoyed a meal at the Soldiers' Rest shortly before heading south via rail to rejoin his unit, and left a detailed description of the building in his postwar memoir:

We went in about noon to the Soldiers Rest, where a couple of hundred others were in the same predicament as myself, awaiting transportation. The Soldiers Rest was a very large building, fitted up by the Government for the accommodation of soldiers passing through the city. A large dining room was attached, and one thousand men could readily have eaten at one time. The fare consisted of boiled pork, bread and coffee, and could be had at any hour of the day or night; and about a score of colored waiters were in constant attendance.[54]

Due to its status as a place of general rendezvous for troops all across the Northern states, notable general officers were often stationed at or passed through the city, exciting not only Harrisburg's citizenry but also its visiting soldiers. Major Generals Darius Couch and Franz Sigel, both of the Department of the Susquehanna, were frequenters in Harrisburg from 1863 to 1864. One evening in 1864, a Northern officer walked into the Jones House only to find Sigel and Couch lounging in the parlor. Sigel played the piano while "[s]ome lady sang like a regular prima donna."[55] Sightings of Couch and other notable general officers were fairly frequent in wartime Harrisburg. "This morning [I] saw Gen Couch," logged volunteer Bently Kutz in his diary on July 15, 1864. "[H]e is a fine looking man."[56]

With the thousands of soldiers who passed through Harrisburg during the war, most had opinions of the city and its people. "Harrisburg seems a real old-fashioned place," observed one artillery lieutenant stationed near the city. "It seems to combine the peculiarities of a city and small village. In the evening the people fill the streets, and the porches are crowded with ladies."[57] "Harrisburg is a Dutch town in every sense of the word, and is at least fifty years behind the times," opined Surgeon D.P. Chamberlin of the 4th Michigan Infantry. "No regularity about streets, houses or anything else, for that matter. The only thing that I admire is [the] real splendid Railroad bridges."[58] Corporal Lyman Beebe of the 151st Pennsylvania found the Keystone State capital to be "a dirty stinking place."[59] On another note, many soldiers took an opportunity during their time in Harrisburg to sightsee. "I saw the grave of John Harris [Sr.] who is buried on the bank of the river under the same tree where the Indians had him tied…ready to burn him," wrote Surgeon James L. Dunn of the 109th Pennsylvania.[60]

The war had an interesting impact on Harrisburg's many businesses. In the decade leading up to the war, the city had seen unprecedented growth, which understandably was stagnated initially by the outbreak of the war. In April 1861, businesses throughout the nation were uncertain what the war meant. However, many Northern businesses soon found a way to turn a profit by obtaining government contracts to supply the military. The task of securing government contracts was made significantly easier for a few select Harrisburgers now that Simon Cameron—who had many ties to the city—was secretary of war, and more often than not, he awarded contracts to his personal friends and acquaintances. Cameron's former banking partner, William Calder Jr. of Harrisburg, was charged with amassing horses and mules for the army. Jacob Eby, another former banking partner of Cameron's, received a number of contracts to supply rations. In one instance in October 1861, Eby received a contract when bidding was opened to supply rations to Camp Cameron, located east of the city. However, two other Harrisburg merchants—George W. Hummel and David McCormick—had submitted bids less than his, Hummel's the cheapest. When McCormick inquired why Hummel did not receive the contract, the commissary replied that "he had positive orders from Washington to give the contract to Mr. Eby, without regard to price."

Perhaps the most notable example of corruption was Cameron's persistent use of the Northern Central Railway as the main route to transport soldiers from Harrisburg to Baltimore. A shareholder and heavy influence in the company, Cameron had bought "large blocks" of the line's stock upon the outbreak of the war, knowing that the railway would be in heavy demand by the military. In several cases, even when the Northern

Central was the longer route, Cameron would prod troops and supplies along that railway. Eventually, Cameron's widespread corruption forced him to resign and instead assume the insignificant post of ambassador to Russia, a steep fall from secretary of war. However unjust his actions were, Cameron did help boost Harrisburg's wartime economy, further solidifying the city as an important railroad hub in the war.

Even without Cameron's antics, Harrisburg's businesses still managed to profit from the war. Upon the outbreak of hostilities, "the shock embarrassed and prostrated manufacturing operations," reported William T. Hildrup, general manager of the Harrisburg Car Factory. "The depression, however, was of brief duration, and little by little a reaction took place, until owing to a large demand for war supplies, a marked business activity prevailed." Heavy wartime taxes weighed down many businesses, but with the increased business prompted by the war, it was still possible to turn a profit.[61] For the many small shops thronging Harrisburg's streets, sales directly to the soldiers proved a lucrative venture. Considering the thousands of soldiers who passed through the city during the war—and counting on homesickness and necessity to drive them to spend—a large market was available for the merchants of Harrisburg, particularly among veteran soldiers as they prepared to return home.

Clothing was commonly recognized as the bestselling product among returning veterans. After months, and in some cases years, of demanding marching, drilling and combat, the uniforms the men had donned throughout their war experience were more often than not in deteriorating condition. "[T]he merchants did a lively and thriving trade," reported Sergeant George F. Sprenger of the 122nd Pennsylvania, "as those of the men who were fortunate enough to be in possession of the essential lucre, soon purchased and donned outfits of new and clean underwear, rapidly ridding themselves of 'the old army duds.'" Harrisburg's shopkeepers quickly caught on to this trend, and in 1865, as many veterans passed through the city en route for home, clothing shops rapidly appeared. One Harrisburger later recalled that in 1865 "every available space on Market street was utilized as a clothing store." These sales to veterans were boosted by another factor: almost all had at least some cash on hand, considering that most were returning to Harrisburg to be paid off. By one account, a member of the 51st Pennsylvania spent "nearly the whole sum" of his $300 pay he received in the shops of Harrisburg, on "a suit of clothing, a gold 'bogus' watch and other jewelry."[62]

With the establishment of Camp Curtin, Harrisburg quickly became a city defined by war. Recruiting flags flew from numerous offices and buildings. Various shops in town sold patriotic products; envelopes, letterhead and all sorts of paper was proclaimed "Union" after a patriotic seal or symbol—often of a flag, a cannon or a woman—was imprinted on it. These were not only of interest to Harrisburg's citizenry but also practically a necessity for incoming soldiers who wished to write home. Numerous military departments set up offices inside the city. Trade at Market Square was interrupted little, and Harrisburg soon settled into the hustle and bustle of a city at war. Reminiscing more than forty years later, Harrisburger Francis Hoy wrote of this much-transformed city:

> *It was a most wonderful place. Our streets were thronged day and night. When war was declared it was a beautiful yet a serious sight to see men coming in companies to volunteer their services to their country. Every day we saw great crowds coming up Market street, with two or three men in front, playing upon violins or banjos, stirring patriotic airs.*[63]

Although patriotic airs were high in April 1861, many in Harrisburg could not help but notice the drastic changes that had occurred in so short a time. It had been just seven months since Prince Edward and his entourage had eyed the surrounding vicinity from the capitol dome. The Dauphin County Agricultural Fairgrounds was then concluding its annual show. Now, in April 1861, Harrisburg—and the fairgrounds in particular—was the center of a great military camp and a place of general rendezvous for thousands of soldiers, the likes of which had not yet been seen in the young nation. For the next four years, Harrisburg and its citizenry were to play an instrumental and constant role in their nation's largest and bloodiest conflict since the founding of the republic.

Chapter 2

Camp Curtin and Its Subsidiaries

For three mortal hours we marked time in the endless march. No halt was ordered; no opportunity was given to ground arms. My friend once lowered his sapling, and stood a moment at parade rest, but the point of a bayonet at his back sharply reminded him that in this sort of circumambulation, there was no rest for the wicked.
—Private Thomas F. Dornblaser, the "Bullring,"
Camp Cameron, near Harrisburg[54]

Largely under the direction of General Edward C. Williams, Major Joseph F. Knipe and Captain Seneca G. Simmons, the Dauphin County Agricultural Fairgrounds were quickly transformed into the largest military training grounds in the North.[65] Camp Curtin itself "occupied the entire space of what is now Fifth street to Seventh street, and from Maclay street to within a very few yards of Reel's lane." The encampment was surrounded on all sides by the "high plank wall" dating from the days of the agricultural fairgrounds. Ridge Road served as the main way of passage from the city to Camp Curtin. Walking Ridge Road by foot was rendered unpleasant not only because of the mile-long tramp from Harrisburg proper to the grounds but also due to the ever-present dust that was stirred up from travel. The preferred way of transportation for civilians visiting the camp was by hack. A business quickly sprang up, and "hackmen," as they were called, conveyed anyone from curious civilians to family and friends of soldiers from Market Street to the camp for a fare of twenty-five cents. During the fall of 1862, while searching for his son, who had been wounded at the Battle of Antietam, American literary giant Oliver Wendell Holmes decided to burn some daylight with a visit to Camp Curtin, and he later noted his journey northward along Ridge Road in a "rickety wagon." While the hacks ran relatively uncontested throughout the war, in July 1865, as the conflict was coming to a close, the Harrisburg City Passenger Railway opened for business. In operation all days of the week except Sunday, the line extended from Third and Walnut Streets north to what later became Maclay Street, then the southern boundary of Camp Curtin. However, persistent troubles with cars derailing plagued the line early on in its existence.[66]

Camp Curtin's original gate stood twenty-five feet east of Ridge Road but was later enlarged to the road. The expanded entryway consisted of three sections: the first, original single gate; the second, a double gate for wagons; and another single gate.[67] The entrance was guarded night and day by sentinels, "who permit no person to pass unless they produce a permit from the proper officer," albeit the full execution of this order was often scarce.[68] Obtaining entrance was relatively easy for most civilians. At times during the war, the camp would be closed to peddlers and pedestrians who attempted to sell food to the soldiers, namely due to rumors that spread through the encampment of poisoned apples, pies and other eatables. Immediately upon entering the gates, situated at the head of the camp was Floral Hall, designated the camp headquarters. The Stars and Stripes flew proudly over the structure. Initially, the building's first floor was "devoted exclusively" to the commissary department, where the "commissary and his clerks are constantly in attendance to deal out the rations to the companies as fast as the proper applications are made." "[T]he piles of provisions in store there we opine, would astonish the eyes of some of our citizens," reported the *Telegraph*. The second story was divided into offices for camp officials. Surrounding Floral Hall was a racetrack, another of the relics from the antebellum fairgrounds. Immediately east of camp headquarters was the Judge's Stand, which had also seen use during the prewar days for contests held on the grounds. This was converted into an office for Captain Seneca Simmons, the camp's first mustering officer.[69]

Camp Curtin's hospital building was hastily erected in late April 1861.[70] The wooden structure was located on the western side of the encampment.[71] When a committee representing the Pennsylvania Nurse Corps visited the hospital on May 17, 1861, the group was "informed that there were at that time thirteen patients—there had never been more than twenty-three—and but one death had occurred from sickness since the camp had

This etching is among the earliest images of Camp Curtin, published in the popular pictorial *Harper's Weekly* on May 11, 1861. Of note in this engraving is the camp headquarters in Floral Hall, adorning the American flag at center. Also visible in the far right background is the State Lunatic Hospital. *Dickinson College Archives and Special Collections.*

been established, and that was before the hospital was erected. Each man is furnished with a clean straw bed, clean sheets and pillow case, clean drawers and shirt when they are received into the hospital. They have three physicians, whose reputation for skill and kindness, as well as experience, is established beyond all doubt."[72] In the fall of 1862, the Ladies' Union Relief Association of Harrisburg were granted permission to erect a small kitchen on the hospital grounds, which was operated daily beginning at 9:00 a.m. by four women from the association who served three day shifts.[73]

The camp hospital was among a number of buildings constructed in the several weeks following Camp Curtin's establishment. A structure was erected in the southwestern corner of camp to house the commissary department, which moved from its cramped quarters in the first story of Floral Hall to this new, more spacious building. The *Patriot* reported that the commissary department "takes up the entire large building, and is very complete." "We visited the Commissary's department, and found barrels of as good crackers as we have ever eaten, of every variety," recounted the committee from the Pennsylvania Nurse Corps that visited the camp on May 17, as well as "bags of coffee piled at least four feet high, barrels and bags of first rate rice, beans in large quantity, sugar, good fresh bread…pork as good as we can purchase in market, a whole fresh beef, butter." Also constructed during this period was a building housing the quartermaster's department, which was located at the head of the camp, immediately east of the gate.[74]

Camp Curtin General Hospital, photographed circa 1864. *Historical Society of Dauphin County.*

Various buildings formerly used at the fairgrounds, including horse and cattle pens, were "thoroughly cleaned, weatherboarded and filled with straw for the accommodation of the troops." Carpenters were put to work "erecting similar structures around the entire enclosure."[75] In August 1861, soldier Thomas Lucas mused that his quarters looked "for all the world like a sheep shed," although he noted that they were "very comfortable except that we have to sleep on the floor."[76] By August 1863, the wear and tear of more than two years' use had left these makeshift barracks in poor condition, and the structures were condemned by a board of survey appointed by the government to examine them. Several weeks later, the barracks were demolished, and in their place were constructed buildings "better suited" to the purpose of housing soldiers.[77]

The area north of camp headquarters at Floral Hall was dominated by a sea of tents. The *Telegraph* detailed that "about a thousand" tents occupied "nearly all the available ground northwest of Floral Hall" shortly after the camp's founding. The *Patriot* estimated that "[s]ome five or six hundred tents are up." Corporal Sidney T. Muffley of the 10th Pennsylvania Infantry

The identity of the first (top) structure at Camp Curtin remains in question due to a conflicting and erroneous original caption. The building was either in use as the building masters' headquarters or the headquarters of the camp commissary department. The photograph below shows another angle of Camp Curtin's General Hospital. This image later served as the model for a popular engraving of the structure (see page 83) that was reprinted in several local histories. *Philip German Scrapbook Collection, Historical Society of Dauphin County.*

wrote that the camp contained thirty-seven rows of tents, "each row being capable of accommodating 130 men." Each tent was floored with an "abundance of clean straw, and look altogether quite comfortable places of habitation," opined the *Telegraph*.[78] Immediately north of the camp was Hoffman's Woods. Confederate prisoners were camped on the western edge of the woods, while out-of-state Yankee soldiers often bivouacked on the woods' eastern limits. Other quarters for Southern captives existed in the northeastern corner of camp.[79] The guardhouse was located in the southeast corner of the camp. When soldiers disobeyed camp protocol or missed the morning roll call, they were placed in the structure as punishment. The thought of imprisonment in the filthy quarters struck fear into many soldiers in Camp Curtin—among the filth were lice. Private Joseph D. Baker of the 57th Pennsylvania wrote home, "[T]he lice are shaking heads…from rafter to rafter—thank providence I have not been in it yet."[80]

When a smallpox epidemic broke out among the camp during the winter of 1862–63, a separate hospital building was constructed at the eastern side of the encampment. There, patients inflicted with the deadly disease were quarantined from the rest of the encampment, just as patients

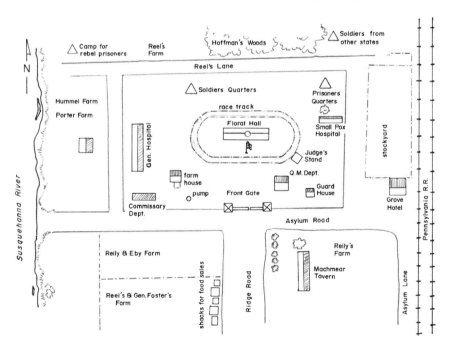

Camp Curtin. *Map by John Heiser.*

with other ailments were separated in the general hospital located on the complete opposite side of the camp. The pandemic had subsided by the summer of 1863, when the smallpox hospital prepared to open its doors to the overwhelming number of wounded soldiers from the bloody Battle of Gettysburg in July 1863. "There is not the least danger of contagion resulting from patients being placed in the building," assured the *Telegraph*, "as the bunks and every article of clothing which the small pox patients used were burned immediately after they left the hospital." The entire building had been "thoroughly cleaned and whitewashed" and was reportedly capable of accommodating "about forty patients."[81]

Camp Curtin's drove yard, where horses and mules would be branded and often quartered, adjoined the camp on its eastern boundary. At the Black Horse Tavern, located along the riverbank near the city's southern limits, horses and mules were examined. A number of Harrisburg "boys" would turn a profit by escorting the mounts that passed the inspection to the Camp Curtin stockyard, wait while the animals were branded and then return with them to the tavern for 50 cents per round trip. "We usually took six horses at a time," recalled Harrisburger Francis Hoy, "riding one and leading the other five." The drove yard contained a portable forge, which was operated by a gentleman whose business it was to brand the horses. "He had an iron rod about eight feet long on the end of which was a plate containing the letters, 'U.S.,'" wrote Hoy. "This was made red hot and pressed against the animal's shoulder or hip."[82]

In late April 1861, shortly after the camp's establishment, twenty-year-old Corporal Sidney T. Muffley of the Curtin Guards from Bellefonte (later Company B, 10th Pennsylvania) penned one of the most comprehensive early accounts of the encampment:

> *Camp Curtin covers about twenty acres of ground, and is surrounded by a high plank wall, built against which are the Barracks for the soldiers. In the centre are thirty seven rows of tents, each row being capable of accommodating 130 men…You could travel to and fro for hours through Camp Curtin and you would not be disgraced with scenes of debauchery so strict are our militia laws, that no soldiers [sic] is permitted to enter camp intoxicated, and none within a certain limit prescribed are permitted to sell soldiers liquor. At the head of the Camp are located the hospital, arsenal, provision house, and officers of the commanding officers of Camp Curtin. Between each row of tents in our canvas city are twenty-five feet of ground for drill which are called streets, and of course each one has a*

name. Our Captain has given the street on which we reside the honorable name of Bellefonte street, and withal we think is the most handsome street in our city of nearly 8,000 inhabitants. Provisions are planty [sic], every soldier has fresh beef, ham, beans, rice, bread, in fact all the solid food that is required to make a man healthy. On Sunday there is a little moderation in the exercises, the soldiers are permitted to attend church, but notwithstanding the fife and drum is ever sounding for that reason Sunday is not so very pleasant. At 5 in the morning the reveille is sounded which calls us to drill for one hour, then after drill we have breakfast[,] two more hours drill, and then the forenoon's work is done, three more in the afternoon and you have the work of each day. At night the lights are all extinguished, the guards relieved and the soldiers retire. The road from the city to camp [Ridge Road] is thronged all hours with soldiers, citizens and hucksters of all kinds, these latter individuals are not permitted to enter the camp of late, by reason of some reports current of the poisoning of several soldiers by eating cakes, &c., purchased from them.[33]*

Camp Curtin frequently experienced overcrowding due to the enormous number of volunteers pouring into the city, and during the course of the war, a number of smaller, subsidiary camps were established nearby. The first recorded subsidiary of Camp Curtin was Camp Greble, an artillery encampment established in June 1861. Following Greble in July 1861 was Camp Cameron, the first of two camps named after the secretary of war and part-time resident of Harrisburg. Details about the camp's founding are scarce, and only one regiment is recorded to have occupied the encampment, the 4th Michigan Infantry. Accounts from the 4th all place the location of this first Camp Cameron a short distance east of Camp Curtin, near the Pennsylvania Railroad and Canal. The 4th only spent five days at Camp Cameron, arriving on June 27 and departing on July 1.[34]

The first substantial subsidiary camp near Harrisburg was established in early August 1861. Colonel Samuel Black's 62nd Pennsylvania Infantry arrived in Harrisburg via rail from Pittsburgh at about 9:00 a.m. on the morning of Sunday, August 4. The war-bound regiment remained in the cars for roughly an hour, until Colonel Black was prepared to form the regiment into column. "[B]ut the time came at last for us to leave the cars and the Boys was glad for we were tired [of] Setting," penned Samuel J. Alexander of the 62nd. Black marched his regiment to the capitol grounds, where they camped for the next several days. "[I]t is a beautiful place very Shady," wrote Alexander. "[A]fter night we went into the capitol to Sleep but it was so hot

Corporal Sidney T. Muffley. While serving as the adjutant of the 184th Pennsylvania later in the war, Muffley visited the studio of Harrisburg photographer LeRue Lemer in Wyeth's Hall, located beside the county courthouse, where this carte-de-vista of Muffley was taken. *U.S. Army Military History Institute.*

that we could not stand it, so the most of us went out and slept on the grass." After three nights of "first rate" slumber on the capitol grounds, Alexander felt "better than I have…for maney years." On the morning of August 6, Black "announced that a place for a camp had been selected on the farm of General Cameron, our much-respected and efficient Secretary of War." Shortly after noon, the regiment departed the capitol complex en route for Cameron's Woods, located roughly two miles east-southeast of Harrisburg.

"The Colonel showed his usual foresight and good judgment in selecting the ground for the camp," opined one Pennsylvanian. "Our tents are pitched in a fine large field from which an excellent crop of rye was cut a short time since; while just alongside there is a beautiful and shady grove which has been used for years by picnic parties from Harrisburg. Within two or three squares, also, we have two fine springs of clear and sparkling water and a pure stream to bathe in. So far we are well fixed." "[W]e have a Woods… to lay around in and a field to drill in so we have entered into a Soldiers life in good earnest," described Alexander. "[T]he Boys are all Busy putting up there tents, and evry thing is very lifely." Within a matter of days, the men of the 62nd were comfortably situated in Cameron's Woods. The site was christened Camp Cameron, in honor of Simon Cameron, on whose property the encampment was located. On August 15, a War Department order officially established Camp Cameron as a "camp of rendezvous and instruction for volunteers."[85]

Life in Camp Cameron was enjoyable and pleasant. "The greatest peace still prevails in the beautiful soldiers' home, 'Camp Cameron,' and all appear full of joy and mirth," reported one member of Black's regiment. "The general health of the regiment is very good, considering the change to which we have all been subjected, from a life at home to a soldier's life in the tented field." "[T]he health of the Regiment is very good so far with the except[ion] of a little of the Diareah," reported Samuel Alexander. As of August 19, only one death had occurred on the premises. "The Camp still remains one of the model camps, as everything is peace and quietness, and the most rigid discipline is forced on any who may be so foolish as to disobey any of the general order," detailed one Pennsylvanian. "There is a prayer meeting conducted in the camp every evening, and really every thing in the camp is almost as quiet as Sunday in old Pitt, as card playing, swearing and all obscene language are entirely forbidden by the Colonel."[86] Samuel Alexander of the 62nd described life in Camp Cameron in a letter to his wife:

I will give you the rules of the camp[.] [T]he Reveille is beat at 5 in the morning when we have to get up to answer Roll call we then have a halfe hour to wash and fresh up we then go out and drill till halfe past 7 we then get Brakefast and at halfe past 9 we go out againe and drill until halfe past 11. We are dismissed until half past 12 Oclock when we are called together for dinner. After that we are dismissed until 4 Oclock when we are called together for Regimental drill and after that we have dress Parade. [T]hen Supper at 7 oclock then we are at liberty to Strole around camp till 9 Oclock then the Role is called and we have to go to bed[.] [W]e are not alowed to leave camp on aney ocasion except on Special Business. [T]hen our pass has to be signed by the Col. [H]e had his quarters in the camp with us and he will not let one of the Officers leave the Camp without a pass[.] [H]e will not alow any Liquor in the camp or any Swearing or

Colonel Samuel Black. *U.S. Army Military History Institute.*

obscene language in the limits of the camp we have preaching in camp evry Sunday we all have to attend[.] [S]o far we have had a methodist minister[.] So you se[e] our Col has a[n] eye to our Spiritual welfare.[87]

The 62nd left Camp Cameron and Harrisburg on August 20 for Baltimore.[88] Despite the departure of its founders, Camp Cameron lived on. The encampment soon became home to a variety of companies and regiments. As of September 21, Camp Cameron was home to 1,223 soldiers.[89] By mid-October, editors from the *Telegraph* estimated that "about thirty-five hundred troops" were quartered in the encampment.[90] "The location of our camp is beautiful with large cultivated farms on either side of us," penned Private Charles M. Rumsey of the 7th Pennsylvania Cavalry, which was quartered in the camp that autumn. A large apple orchard was situated nearby, but by October, it had been cleaned of its fruit. Also located near the encampment was the Dauphin County poorhouse or almshouse. "I visited it once & the most dirty place you ever saw is nothing compared with it," detailed Rumsey.[91]

Among the regiments forming in the camp during the fall of 1861 were the 7th and 9th Pennsylvania Cavalry. When Private Thomas F. Dornblaser of the 7th arrived in Harrisburg, his company was ordered to march for Camp Cameron. "This was our first march," noted Dornblaser, "and in some respects it was a *forced march*, as some of the boys preferred to go in hacks, but that was unsoldier-like and contrary to orders. With a huge bundle on each shoulder, and an occasional umbrella raised to break the rays of a warm October sun, we footed it through the dusty highway to Camp Cameron." As Dornblaser and his company entered Camp Cameron, "it seemed as if every tent in that vast encampment had emptied itself, to swell the crowd of spectators that lined the street on either side." The Clinton County native was convinced that the company's "manly bearing" left enough of a favorable impression upon regimental commander Colonel George Wynkoop to assign the company quarters at the center of the regiment's encampment. "A row of sixteen edge-tents was allotted to the company—six men to occupy each tent," recalled Dornblaser. "A marquee, a large field tent, stood apart at the head of the company, which was occupied by the captain and his two lieutenants. Loads of straw were hauled into camp for bedding, to which we helped ourselves freely…In a tent whose ground measurement was seven by eight, with a ridge pole nine feet from the ground, there was not much room left in which to entertain strangers, after six of us crawled in one top of a half dozen armfuls of straw and twice as many bundles of clothing."[92]

Private Thomas F. Dornblaser.
From Dornblaser's My Life Story for Young and Old, *1930.*

The twenty-year-old Dornblaser and his comrades soon became acquainted with the poor quality of rations they would receive in Camp Cameron. The hardtack issued to them was among the stalest of that infamous cracker. "The kind issued to our regiment during the first ten days," penned Dornblaser, "were the old navy crackers, stale, worm-eaten, and hard as a brick. They were doubtless left over as a surplus from previous wars, and were now issued by the commissary department to break in new recruits. If you attempted to crush one with your fist, you were likely to injure your knuckles more than you would the cracker." Disgruntled with their daily fare, one evening several hundred men of the 7th "rushed from their tents, each loaded with forty rounds of ammunition, and with a concert of action that was truly wonderful, they were seen in the starlight charging with furious impetuosity upon the headquarters of the commissary department, fairly burying the suspected officials beneath a stormy bombardment of *hard-tack*." Their unconventional method of protest proved successful, and several days later, "the old navy iron-clads" were exchanged for more tasteful, "fresh" hardtack, complemented by a two-pound loaf of "soft bread," issued to each individual soldier every five days for the rest of his tenure in Camp Cameron.[93]

The stringent discipline with which Colonel Black originally directed the encampment remained evident throughout Camp Cameron's existence. However, punishments and consequences had changed drastically by the fall of 1861. Striking fear into the heart of every soldier who ever entered the encampment was the so-called Bullring. Private Charles Rumsey of the 7th Cavalry informed his sister, "I would not be obliged to walk that Bullring for the best farm in Sullivan." Located at a large tree on the "highest eminence in camp," soldiers violating camp protocol were forced to continuously pace around the tree for several hours. Culprits would first be taken to camp headquarters, where if their excuse were to be found unsatisfactory to the camp commandant, they would be ordered to the Bullring. Before reaching their dreaded destination, the scalawags would be marched at the point of bayonet to the camp wood yard, where "each, according to specific directions, shouldered a stick of cord-wood," recalled Dornblaser, who was once unfortunate enough to be caught outside camp without written permission.[94] He wrote:

> From here we marched by twos at right-shoulder shift, to the brow of the hill, where we met a goodly number of our comrades treading the wine-press of repentance, and as we joined the procession they fairly shouted for joy. The ring, so conspicuous in our memory, was situated on the brow of a hill by a the public highway, in size about like the arena in a circus, well guarded by muskets, and surrounded on that Sabbath afternoon by as many spectators as witnessed at one time the bull-fights in the Coliseum at Rome…For three mortal hours we marked time in the endless march. No halt was ordered; no opportunity was given to ground arms. My friend once lowered his sapling, and stood a moment at parade rest, but the point of a bayonet at his back sharply reminded him that in this sort of circumambulation, there was no rest for the wicked.[95]

After his mortifying and exhausting forced march around the Bullring, Dornblaser and his fellow culprits were "conducted by a heavy escort to the guard-house, to spend the night in *durance vile*." The Clinton County farmer may have thought that his punishment could get no worse than his treatment at the Bullring, but he soon found conditions at Camp

Cameron's ramshackle guardhouse to be even poorer. "There was no room in the board shanty to lie down, nor to sit, so we leaned against the wall," Dornblaser recalled.

> *The floor was covered with three and four thicknesses of legs and arms tangled and twisted into all sorts of shapes. Mutterings and blasphemies rose at intervals, like a blue blaze, from the ulterior strata. New recruits hourly arriving from the slums of Harrisburg, were forced into the guardhouse by the end of the musket, and tumbling over the slumbering heaps of humanity gave occasion for additional wailing and gnashing of teeth. One unconquerable Hibernian determined not to endure any longer such bitter humiliation. Taking a rope in hand, he mounted one of the rafters, fastened the rope around his neck, and swore that he would hang himself. The guards, wishing to avoid the trouble of burying him, took him down, and cooled his ardor by tying him to a tree till morning.*[96]

For those who resisted or misbehaved at the Bullring or in the guardhouse, further punishment awaited. Typically, a disorderly soldier was forced to stand on or was tied to a barrel.[97] Compared to some military establishments, Camp Cameron was not atypical; however, when compared to the lax discipline exercised at Camp Curtin, regulations in Camp Cameron seemed tyrannical. Private Benjamin Steiner of the 76th Pennsylvania, which was quartered in the encampment during the fall of 1861, informed his brother of the camp's stringent discipline:

> [W]e dare not fight at [a]ll no ads what any one calls us[.] About one week ago Jake [I]rwin called me and Hen [b]oth sons of B—s and [I] had my Butcher knife in my hand eating my dinner and all that kept me from strikeing him in the face was the laws that [I] am under…[Y]ou would think it very hard if you could not even get outside of the camp without a pass signed By your captain and By the agutant and the colnal and then if you ant in By five oclock you will be put in the guard house for twenty four hours and half of that time you will have to walk the Bull ring and if you resist you will have to stand on a barl for six [h]ours and then you dare not say one sausy word to the captain as he will Buck and gag you that is take the Baynet of your gun and tie it in your mouth and tie your hands behind your back and make you sit down on your bunkers till he is ready do let you up.[98]

Writing on October 22, 1861, one member of Company D, 7th Pennsylvania Cavalry, described Camp Cameron as being "divided into three different departments as follows: one part is called Col. [George] Wynkoop's [7th Pennsylvania Cavalry] Regiment, which contains about fifteen hundred men; the second is the artillery department…and the third is [Colonel E.C.] William's [sic] department, which contains about two thousand men, making in the aggregate about five thousand men."[99] Although the estimates of the camp's strength are likely inaccurate, this account does provide important insight into the makeup of Camp Cameron. Wynkoop's "department" held the twelve companies composing the 7th Pennsylvania Cavalry, and the artillery "department" likely refers to another subsidiary camp adjoining Camp Cameron, Camp Greble. The reference to Williams's "department" denotes Colonel Edward C. Williams—the Harrisburg resident who as a state militia general had played an instrumental role in the founding of Camp Curtin in April 1861—as well as his newly christened 9th Pennsylvania Cavalry Regiment. Williams and his 9th Pennsylvania departed Camp Cameron on November 25, destined for the Western Theater.[100] Wynkoop's 7th Cavalry followed in Williams's footsteps, proceeding to the Western Theater the following month, where both units would serve for the remainder of the war.

Another unit that occupied Camp Cameron for several weeks during the fall of 1861 was the 76th Pennsylvania Infantry, commonly known as the "Keystone Zouaves." Perhaps one of the best descriptions of life in Camp Cameron after Black's departure is contained in a September 23 letter written by a member of Company F:

Our company is now located in Camp Cameron, about two miles from Harrisburg, in a beautiful situation on the border of a piece of woodland. It is laid out rather irregularly, owing to the unevenness of the ground. There are now fourteen companies of infantry, five companies of cavalry, and one battery of artillery in camp. Seven of the infantry companies belong to Col. Powers' Keystone Zouave Regiment [76th Pennsylvania Infantry.] Three more companies will arrive this week, when the full number of companies will be in camp. All the men belonging to the Zouave Regiment are now uniformed, and we expect by the last of the week to be fully equipped with new tents and camp furniture. The entire camp is under the control of Major [Thomas] Williams, 5th Artillery, U.S.A. He has established strict military discipline throughout.—Reveille beats at daybreak; Breakfast Call at 6 A.M.; Drill Call at 7¾ A.M., when

This photograph of two soldiers in the 76th Pennsylvania Infantry, one identified as Private John M. Knox of Company F, was taken in Camp Cameron on November 5, 1861. *U.S. Army Military History Institute.*

we have squad drill for one hour. Drill Call again at 9 A.M., when we have company drill for an hour and a half, in a field about one-fourth of a mile distant from camp. Dinner call at 12 M. Police Call at 1 P.M. Drill Call again at 3 P.M. After drilling for two hours we have dress parade, and at 6 P.M. guard mounting. Tattoo beats at 8 P.M., and at 8½, Taps are sounded, when all lights must be extinguished and the men are in their quarters. Major W. has also ordered that as soon as a competent officer can be obtained, an officers' drill and recitation in military tactics will be had daily.[101]

By December 1861, the 7th Pennsylvania Cavalry was the only unit remaining in Camp Cameron. No longer was there a pressing need for the camp, and it was announced that the encampment would be "broken up" when the 7th departed. On March 19, 1862, a public auction was held in which "all the lumber etc., composing the camp"—roughly 200,000 feet of lumber—was auctioned off by the U.S. Army.[102]

In June 1861, Major Thomas Williams of the 5th U.S. Artillery established Camp Greble about two miles east-southeast of Harrisburg, adjoining what would later become Camp Cameron. "I have established a camp of instruction here, and called it 'Camp Greble' in honor of our gallant friend who fell at Bethel," Williams wrote to his wife. Lieutenant Colonel John Trout Greble had been killed at the Battle of Big Bethel, the first Regular Army officer to be killed during the war. Camp Greble's first commander was Lieutenant Colonel Thomas W. Sherman of the 5th Artillery. Sherman—a future general in the Union army—departed Harrisburg in late July, leaving Williams in command.[103] Second Lieutenant Henry Sanford Gansevoort of the 5th described the camp in a letter home written on September 10:

The camp is about a mile and a half from town, and situated on the level top of a broad hill that slopes away towards a small stream in the rear, and undulates somewhat at the front. The Susquehanna, at the distance of about a mile, gleams in the sunlight through lines of forest; and on all sides in the distance appear white tents, and ring the bugles, of volunteer forces... There are about a hundred and fifty men in camp; and as fast as they are prepared they will be sent off in a battery of that number with six guns.[104]

Although the camp was located on a hilltop, "the dew after seven in the evening is very heavy," penned Gansevoort, "and boots and shoes suffer, albeit they be clogs." Recruits continually filtered into the camp. "There are now here, the major [Williams] commanding, adjutant, surgeon, a captain, one first and five or six second lieutenants," Gansevoort recorded. "The remaining officers are now recruiting." The camp was always bustling during the daytime with incessant drilling. "Our studies are very severe here," he detailed, "and are pursued on the West Point system. They comprise

Major Thomas Williams. A West Pointer, Williams later rose to the rank of brigadier general of volunteers and was killed in action at Baton Rouge on August 5, 1862. *MOLLUS-MASS Collection, U.S. Army Military History Institute.*

the manual of light artillery, but will soon extend to heavy artillery and ordnance."[105] Gansevoort wrote on September 20:

> *We are engaged in drilling in marching movements, and at the guns. I take to a soldier's life and duties naturally. At reveille, which is at daybreak, we rise, and in turn, each week, we attend to the policing, or having the*

camp cleaned, which is done under the charge of a sergeant by the guard of the day before. At six we breakfast under an open tent, all together. At six and three quarters the bugle sounds from the distant hill for drill. We then proceed to quarters, and after inspecting the men, who have been already formed into detachments by the sergeants, we each take a detachment to the piece or to the field. At eight the recall is sounded, the signal to cease drilling. After this the sergeants' call, and at nine o'clock the call for another drill which ceases at half-past ten. At eleven the officers drill,—properly on horseback, but, as we have not our horses, on foot. At twelve drill ceases, and the men are called by bugle to dinner. At one we drill, and at that time there is another "policing" of the camp. At three another drill till half-past four; and at half-past five parade and guard-mounting. At nine, tattoo and taps; and but for the clank of sabre, and the tread of armed sentinels, the camp is silent till daybreak. Now, all this is very severe; but such is the discipline, and the power given to the officers over the men in the regular service, that there is an excitement and satisfaction in doing one's duty, and doing it well…There is a fullness of health produced by the regularity of meals and exercise, that is truly enjoyable. We shall soon be mounted, and then we shall enjoy it much more.[106]

By November 1861, horses had arrived in Camp Greble, allowing officers to drill in riding. "This is not any Broadway equestrianism," Gansevoort explained, "but a bare-back drill on horses that are rougher than any I had hoped to meet. I have not been thrown yet, although with the quick turns of the drill I expect to be. We are drilled by a graduate of West Point, and I hope soon to be as familiar with a horse as I am now with some other requisites of a soldier's life." Sure enough, several days later, Gansevoort was thrown from his horse. "We ride every day new horses, very rough, and sometimes only half broken, which belong to the batteries," he lamented. "There is a parallelogram about two hundred feet long, and fifty feet wide, in which we ride; turning squarely in the trot and walk, but in the gallop performing a species of ellipse. The horses are ridden without any saddle; and it is as much as one's life is worth, sometimes, to mount them."[107]

Camps Cameron and Greble were located close enough to each other that they shared the same "general office tent." Often soldiers quartered within viewed the two encampments as one. Major Williams of the 5th assumed the role of commandant of Camp Cameron sometime shortly after Colonel Black and his 62nd Pennsylvania departed the camp in August 1861. Williams had left Harrisburg by October 2, assigned to command of Fort Hatteras,

Lieutenant Henry Sanford Gansevoort. After departing Harrisburg in early 1862, Gansevoort was later promoted to colonel of the 13th New York Cavalry. *MOLLUS-MASS Collection, U.S. Army Military History Institute.*

North Carolina. With Williams's departure, Captain Truman Seymour of Battery C, 5th U.S.—a veteran of the infamous Fort Sumter conflict who had arrived in Harrisburg in late September—was placed in command of Camp Cameron.[108] The Vermont native would later serve as a brigadier general in the Army of the Potomac, but during the fall of 1861, he was relegated to command of the seemingly insignificant Camp Cameron. During his tenure as commander of the encampment, Seymour quickly earned a reputation as a severe disciplinarian. Sergeant John A. Porter of the 76th Pennsylvania, in Camp Cameron, recalled that "our Commander, Captain Seymore [sic] of the Regular Army…was a great disciplinarian and ruled us with a rod of iron as we thought, but no more so than was for our good and that of the services. His eagle eye was upon us and he saw to it that we did our whole duty."[109] Others had a less favorable opinion of the stringent Regular Army officer.[110] Nevertheless, the citizenry of Harrisburg quickly grew fond of the 5th Artillery. Wrote the editors of the *Telegraph*:

> *Three companies of this fine regiment of regulars…are quartered at Camp Greble…under the command of Capt. Seymour, one of the most competent officers in the army. Their parade through the city yesterday* [December 13] *elicited much praise, not only for the fine healthy appearance of the men, but for the proficiency in drill, and good appointments generally. The men are comfortably lodged at camp, and no regiment in the service is better provided with everything calculated for efficient action than the Fifth Artillery. Young men, who desire to enter the service, would do well to consider the advantages of enrolling themselves in this fine regiment.*[111]

Camp Greble's barracks (which quartered the artillerymen during the winter of 1861–62) consisted of three stables, three shanties, two hospital buildings, a guardhouse, a storehouse, one set of quarters, several huts and a shed (which was blown down).[112] However formidable this description sounds, the buildings provided little defense against harsh winter weather. "The weather is cold, and the wind lets us know that a mere canvas is but a poor shelter," lamented Lieutenant Gansevoort.[113] Throughout the fall and winter of 1861 and into early 1862, batteries departed Camp Greble after filling their ranks. By early March, Captain Henry V. DeHart had assumed command of Camp Greble as the last elements of the 5th Artillery prepared to depart. In late March, the camp was disbanded. On May 8, 1862, the U.S. Army conducted a public auction of Camp Greble's buildings, "used as barracks this winter by the 5th Artillery."[114]

Calls in late July and August 1862 for volunteers to serve a term of nine months brought thousands of men into Camp Curtin. The captain of the first nine-month company to be sworn in, Harrisburger F. Asbury Awl, received orders to "proceed to the fields north of Camp Curtin," where he would establish "a camp suitable for the accommodation of troops that were expected to arrive in large numbers at the seat of government." Awl christened the site Camp Simmons in honor of the late Colonel Seneca G. Simmons of the 5th Pennsylvania Reserves, a Harrisburg resident recently killed in action on the Virginia Peninsula.[115] Born in Windsor, Vermont, on December 27, 1808, Seneca Galusha Simmons entered Captain Alden Partridge's Military Academy, then located in Middletown, Connecticut, in 1826 and graduated in 1829. Later that same year, he received an appointment from President Andrew Jackson to the U.S. Military Academy at West Point, from which he graduated in 1834. Brevetted a second lieutenant in the 7th Infantry after he left West Point, Simmons served in various coastal surveys and engineering positions. In August 1834, Simmons married Elmira Adelaide of Harrisburg. The couple had four children, all born at military posts where their father was on active duty. Simmons's first son, Charles Francis, was born in Augusta, Maine, while his father was conducting a coastal survey of the Pine Tree State. In late 1837, Simmons was appointed aide-de-camp to Brevet Brigadier General Matthew Arbuckle, commanding the Department of the Southwest. The Vermont native spent nearly five years in this capacity at Fort Gibson, located in what was then the Indian Territory (later Oklahoma). At Fort Gibson, sons Douglas Frederick and Edward Courtney were born in 1838 and 1840, respectively.

After serving briefly with his regiment in the concluding actions of the Second Seminole War (also known as the Florida War) during the spring of 1842, Simmons was stationed at Fort Pike, Louisiana, where his fourth and final child, daughter Elmira Adelaide, was born on his thirty-fourth birthday. In 1843, Simmons was detailed for recruiting duty at Syracuse, New York. In Syracuse, Simmons, his family and "a large dog named Bob" rented half of a house belonging to Mr. Stephen Smith. In early 1847, during the Mexican-American War, Simmons was ordered from recruiting duty at Syracuse to the front as an assistant commissary and quartermaster at Matamoras, Mexico. His family, meanwhile, moved to Fort Columbus on Governors Island, New York, where Simmons's third son, Edward Courtney, died. Promoted to captain on February 16, 1847, Simmons "took part in the memorable march of the United States Army to the city of Mexico and distinguished himself at the battle of Huamantla, October 12, 1847."

Colonel Seneca G. Simmons.
*MOLLUS-MASS Collection, U.S.
Army Military History Institute.*

Shortly after the war with Mexico had concluded, the West Point graduate found himself once again battling Seminole Indians in Florida from 1849 to 1850.[116]

Come 1861, Simmons was on leave of absence with his family in Harrisburg. His first son, Charles Francis, had died at Pottsville in March 1856. His second son, Douglas, passed away at Harrisburg in September 1860. By the outbreak of the war, Simmons was left with only his wife and daughter. Adding another tragic twist to Simmons's life was a constraining injury he had received while on the frontier. More than a decade earlier, while stationed at Fort Leavenworth, Kansas, in 1850, one of his knees was "frightfully crushed, and the wound, after some years of intense suffering, resulted in permanent lameness; but not to such an extent as to unfit him entirely for duty." Simmons nevertheless saw various service after his injury, ranging from recruiting duty performed on crutches to assuming command of the frontier garrison Fort Arbuckle. However, when his regiment was ordered to Utah, Simmons obtained a furlough and returned home to his family in Harrisburg.[117]

As thousands of volunteers rushed to Harrisburg in April 1861, Governor Curtin personally appealed to Simmons, requesting him to organize, train and muster in the troops at Camp Curtin. By that time, Simmons had been on leave of absence nearly two years. "Captain Simmons appreciated the situation and was ready to comply with Governor Curtin's request." However, the Regular Army officer could not do so without direct authorization from the secretary of war, who happened to be Curtin's avowed political enemy, Simon Cameron. Due entirely to the "bad feeling" between the two Pennsylvania politicians, Cameron initially rejected Curtin's request for Simmons's service. Curtin, however, bypassed his old rival and went directly to President Lincoln, who ordered the detail of Simmons for duty in Harrisburg.[118]

Simmons served as the camp's first mustering officer for the first regiments formed in the camp. "His appearance at Camp Curtin was the signal for the reign of order," read one postwar account. "Companies were formed, drilled and disciplined by his personal direction. He drilled drill-masters, who in turn drilled awkward squads...He was everywhere in every department at Camp Curtin, seeing to the proper appointments in its commissary and quartermaster's departments, directing the storage of the vast supplies arriving."[119] Simmons was offered and accepted the colonelcy of the 5th Pennsylvania Reserves (34th Pennsylvania Volunteers) in June 1861. Captain and future general John Irvin Gregg had initially been elected the regiment's colonel but resigned after receiving an appointment as a captain in the Regular Army. Despite being "personally unknown to any of the officers of that body," Simmons's experience and nearly thirty years of military service made him a well-respected soldier. "Col. Simmons had been in the service for many years," admonished one member of the 5th Reserves, "and is a regular graduate of West Point."[120]

A year later, in June 1862, Simmons and the men of the 5th Reserves found themselves falling back on the Richmond Peninsula after a series of demoralizing defeats. Engaged in the Battle of Mechanicsville on June 25 and the Battle of Gaines's Mill on June 27, Simmons emerged unscathed from both. After Brigadier General John F. Reynolds was captured napping after Gaines's Mill on June 28, command of the 1st Brigade devolved on Simmons. However, the Vermont native was mortally wounded and captured at the Battle of Glendale (also known as Frayser's Farm and

Charles City Crossroads) while "leading the First brigade with unexampled valor."[121] Nearly twenty years later, Simmons's widow learned the details of her husband's last moments from Oliver M. Doyle, the Confederate surgeon who tended to him:

> *I was told that Col. Simmons fell in front of our part of the line, and as our line advanced, he was taken up and brought to the field hospital by my ambulance corps. He was wounded by a minnie ball, through the liver and lung, and died, I think, the second day. I treated him the best possible under the circumstances, and had him buried as decently as could be done there at such a time. He was reported by our officers and men as acting conspicuously brave on that sanguinary field, as being the cause, in their opinion, of that part of the Federal line standing as long as it did. That report did much towards stimulating a greater desire on our part to do all that was possible for a brave but fallen foe. Before death he thanked us sincerely for our attentions. He gave to some one of our party…a gold watch, a picture of his wife, and I think $60 of gold coin, with the request that the watch and picture…be sent to his wife.*[122]

Doyle's letter arrived twenty years after the fact, however. Elmira Simmons first received positive confirmation of her husband's death several weeks later in the form of two letters—one from Colonel Joseph W. Fisher, who had been promoted to command of Simmons's 5th Reserves upon the latter's death, and the other from Simmons's division commander, Brigadier General George A. McCall, who penned his letter from a Richmond prison. While both letters—McCall's dated July 15 and Fisher's dated July 21—varied in accuracy, both confirmed Elmira Simmons's worse fears.[123] Until her death in 1886, she received a thirty-dollar widow's pension each month.[124] In honor of the fallen Harrisburg resident, Grand Army of the Republic (GAR) Post No. 116 was named the Colonel S.G. Simmons Post.

Camp Simmons itself was located immediately north of Camp Curtin. Contemporary accounts indicate that the camp was largely considered an extension of Camp Curtin. Harrisburg resident Francis Hoy, who was part of Captain Awl's "First City Zouaves," which had founded the camp, later noted, "Camp Simmons lasted only a short time and it finally became part of Camp Curtin."[125] Throughout August 1862, a total of sixteen nine-month regiments were raised (122nd through 137th Pennsylvania Volunteers). For the most part, these units were quartered in Camps Curtin or Simmons on their way to the field. Scarcely had the nine-month units cleared out when a large wave of three-year cavalry companies arrived in Camp Simmons. Already overcrowded and "much congested," the alarming prospect of the soon-to-be-arriving mounts cramming into Camp Simmons served as cause for the cavalrymen to establish another campsite farther north—Camp McClellan, named in honor of former Army of the Potomac commander Major General George B. McClellan, relieved from his post just days earlier.[126]

On November 10, men of the 16th and 17th Pennsylvania Cavalry trekked northward from Camp Simmons to their new campsite about two miles north of Harrisburg.[127] The Pennsylvanians arrived at Camp McClellan at about 1:00 p.m., "all very tired." Pitching tents at once, the men had a chance to take in the attractive scenery surrounding the camp. Private Samuel E. Cormany of the 16th confided in his diary that the "[c]amp has beautiful country surrounding it—and at once strikes one as being romantic in appearance."[128] Joining the 16th and 17th in Camp McClellan was the 18th Pennsylvania Cavalry. Companies B, C, D, E, I and K all moved north from Camp Simmons to Camp McClellan on November 13. Companies A, F, G and H remained in Camp Howe at Pittsburgh until the evening of November 23, when they departed for Harrisburg, arriving early the following morning. After remaining at the depot until sunrise, the contingent marched to Camp McClellan. Overall, the war-bound cavaliers found conditions at their new encampment generally worse than they had experienced at Camp Howe. Private William H. Martin of Company A detailed in a letter home to his wife that he "was not very well satisfied when [I] first arrived here." He added that "we have not got as comfortable quarters as we had in pittsburgh as our tents are made of linen and we have to lay on the ground on straw with five in one tent...[O]ur grub is not as plenty nor as good as it was at pittsburgh." Despite his grievances, the cavalier still admitted that Camp McClellan was "a nice place...for a camp."[129]

The three cavalry regiments were rapidly initiated into military life as they underwent a daily routine of exacting drills. Initially, the rank and file "cheerfully accepted" the rigorous routine; however, the drills soon became "monotonous" and "were regarded by some as superfluous and unnecessary." "We have plenty of exercise," mused Martin. The twenty-eight-year-old cavalryman detailed, "[W]e have to drill on foot from 6 oclock in the morning till half past seven from ten till half eleven from 1 till half 2 [and] dress parade at 4 in the afternoon." Little news regarding the progress of the war reached Camp McClellan, but what the men did manage to glean was positive. "[A]ll that we hear goes in our favor," wrote Private Peter Boyer of the 17th. This, combined with the monotony of drill, increased the unrest of the cavalrymen within the camp; many feared that the war might conclude before they even took to the field. "Everything moves on slowly yet surely as if there was still something to be done," voiced a frustrated Private Samuel Cormany of the 16th Pennsylvania—"a little more preparation, and still a little more."[130] Consistent and arduous drill was combined with strict discipline to make Camp McClellan particularly unappealing. "[W]e have very strict orders here any person being found more than a mile from camp without leave from headquarters the punishment is death," Martin penned.[131] Wrote Private Henry Moyer of the 17th:

> *The discipline of the camp was very strict. Possibly not too strict from a military standpoint. But some of the men considered it too strict for convenience, especially when off duty. They could hardly see the need of remaining in camp so closely when there were opportunities of comfort and enjoyment outside. Because of the strict enforcement and regulations prescribed by the commanding officer and because of the many attractions of a social character in the city of Harrisburg so near the camp, the running of the camp guard was often practiced successfully and many were the stories told of narrow escapes from arrest. Of course occasionally some would fall into the hands of the patrol and had to suffer the consequences.*[132]

Despite the strict discipline, the plundering of private property still took place near the camp, similar to what occurred around Camp Curtin. "In the vicinity of [C]amp McClellan…the acts and the thefts of the soldiers have been most disgraceful," reported the *Telegraph*. "Turkeys, chickens, fruit, fences and other moveable property disappear every night, and if protests are offered to those thus guilty, blows and death are threatened in return."[133] Also reminiscent of Camp Curtin were the peddlers who sold various foods to the soldiers. "[I]t is no wonder that some families suffer at home the way that men spend their money here for apples[,] cakes and pies when they are better off without," Martin wrote. "[I] believe that the majority of the Company spend about one half of their money for such trash as this[.] [T]here is a very good chance to spend money here if one was so minded as there are more or less peddlars in camp every day."[134]

While in Camp McClellan, the rank and file of all three cavalry regiments received horses, sabres and various pieces of horse equipment. For the most part, their mounts came from the Camp Curtin drove yard. "There we went into a pen among about 500 horses, they were all loose, and caught 103 horses and brought them to camp…with rope halters," recorded Private

Jacob Beidler of the 16th. "Many of the horses we had received had never been ridden before," noted Private Henry Moyer of the 17th. "There was rearing and kicking, running and jumping, lying down and falling down, men thrown by their horses, kicked and getting hurt in various ways…All sorts of mishaps occurred, which caused a great deal of discomfort and amusement at times." Private William Martin informed his wife that the horses "are nothing to brag of[.] [S]ome are good and some are not so good." With their mounts now in hand, the cavalrymen were required to make two daily trips through Harrisburg to water their horses in the Susquehanna River.[135] Complaints about reckless riding by some of the horsemen through the city quickly arose. On one Sunday in the city, "about the time the different congregations were dismissed, and the street crossings were crowded with people," several cavalrymen "came dashing along Third street at regular Gilpin speed, rushing as if the rebels were behind them." This wild riding was against both War Department orders and city ordinance. The *Telegraph* proclaimed that "unless the city ordinance is enforced, some of the dashing cavalry officers will make a race course of the streets of Harrisburg."[136] After spending less than a month in Camp McClellan, the three cavalry regiments departed the camp. The 16th and 17th Pennsylvania exited Camp McClellan piecemeal in late November and early December.[137] The 18th was the last to depart the camp, leaving the city on December 8.[138] After the 18th's departure, Camp McClellan was apparently disbanded, having existed for less than a month.

In mid-October 1862, a draft began throughout the commonwealth after it had failed to meet another quota for volunteers from President Lincoln. By December, a total of fifteen regiments had been formed—these units would also serve for nine-month terms. A number of the drafted regiments formed in Camp Simmons in November and December 1862 before departing to garrison duty at various coastal sites in Virginia and North and South Carolina. Upon their return from the field, many of these drafted units arrived in Camp Simmons in July 1863, where they were mustered out and paid. Lieutenant Colonel Joseph F. Ramsey, commanding a battalion of militia raised earlier that summer in response to the "emergency," had command of Camp Simmons at the time.[139]

Another subsidiary located nearby Camp Curtin was Camp Russell, named for Pennsylvania adjutant general A.L. Russell. Little is known about how or exactly when Camp Russell was established. The earliest account of the encampment dates from November 1862, when the 151st Pennsylvania was quartered there.[140] When Harrisburg was threatened by

Colonel Charles Somers Smith, Gray Reserves, 32nd Pennsylvania Militia. *From Latta's History of the First Regiment Infantry National Guard of Pennsylvania, 1912.*

Confederate invasion in June 1863, Colonel Charles Somers Smith and his 32nd Pennsylvania Militia—the "Gray Reserves" of Philadelphia—rushed to Harrisburg and were quartered in Camp Russell. The Philadelphians had been "hustled into Camp Curtin" upon their arrival in Harrisburg, only "to be disgusted with its dirt and foul smell." Smith defiantly marched his Philadelphians out of filthy Camp Curtin to nearby Camp Russell, described as "near the canal," which indicates that Russell was situated somewhere east of Camp Curtin. Another member of the Gray Reserves penned a letter to the *Philadelphia Press*, providing a more definitive description and explaining that Camp Russell was located "a short distance below Camp Curtin, on the line of the railroad," which would place the encampment southeast of Camp Curtin, alongside the railroad and canal.[141]

During the fall of 1862, a camp occupied by two companies was located "near" the Cotton Mill at the city's northern boundary. The soldiers within the camp christened the site Camp Haley after Mrs. Sara Haley, the daughter of late Harrisburger Jacob M. Haldeman. "Mrs. H. has been very liberal to the soldiers, and has allowed no opportunity to pass by where she could minister to the wants of the sick or wounded," detailed the *Telegraph*. "The officers and men of Camp Haley have conferred a just compliment upon a worthy lady." In all probability, the two companies that were quartered at Camp Haley were Captain DeWitt C. James's "Warren County Rifles," officially designated Independent Company C, and Captain Wellington Jones's Independent Infantry Company—both Pennsylvanian units. James's company had been raised with the intention of joining the 145th Pennsylvania; however, that regiment completed organization before the company could report for duty. Mustered into service on September 4, 1862, as an independent company, the outfit arrived in Harrisburg shortly thereafter. Captain James was later designated provost marshal of the city.[142] Located near Camp Haley was Camp Sands. Named for Camp Curtin commandant Captain William A. Sands, the encampment was established during the winter of 1862–63 to accommodate additional drafted companies. Camp Sands was located on the riverbank, south of Camp Curtin but north of Harrisburg proper. It was host to a number of companies (primarily drafted men) throughout the winter of 1862–63. In early March 1863, the camp was "broken up and the men removed to Camp Curtin."[143]

In June 1863, Captain James S. Brisbin—detailed as chief of cavalry of the Department of the Susquehanna—established a cavalry camp east of Harrisburg, near present-day Penbrook. There, several cavalry companies raised in response to the Confederate invasion were organized. "The camp is not very large at present," reported the *Telegraph* on June 24, "but cavalrymen are coming in daily who will swell the numbers now on the ground." The camp eventually became known as Camp Couch.[144] Another temporary camp established during the summer of 1863 was Camp Yahoo, located in Harris Park along the riverbank near the Cumberland Valley Railroad bridge. Occupied by the 23rd New Jersey for only several days, the encampment was located opposite Bridgeport Heights, the towering eminence across the Susquehanna that was then bustling with activity as fortifications were being constructed to defend the city. "With an unobstructed view of the river, and the [Bridgeport] heights on the other side, the men here can amuse themselves for hours, looking through a spy-glass at the movements of the men on the hills beyond," described the editors of the *Telegraph*.[145]

Situated above downtown Harrisburg on North Second Street was Camp Hinks, named for General Edward Winslow Hincks, who had served briefly in Harrisburg on the administrative level. Interestingly enough, in official records, Camp Hinks did not retain General Hincks's original spelling of his name. According to Harrisburg resident Francis Hoy, the camp "was situated on North Second street, occupying part of what is now Briggs, Forster and Green Streets." Known throughout the city as the "Veteran Reserve Corps Camp," the site, as its alias notes, was occupied by men of the Veteran Reserve Corps. This corps was earmarked for men injured too seriously to return to their old regiments, and therefore they played noncombatant roles. The primary occupant of Camp Hinks was the 16th Regiment Veteran Reserve Corps. Parts of the regiment had been stationed in Harrisburg as early as the summer of 1863, and from August 1864 through June 1865, a detachment of the unit was always posted in Harrisburg. Surviving records indicate that several companies occupied Camp Hinks on a sporadic basis during that period—the earliest mention of Camp Hinks within the records of the 16th Regiment occurs in May 1865. However, Harrisburg newspapers mention "barracks" belonging to the regiment on Second Street as of December 1864, which implies that Camp Hinks may have been in operation as early as late 1864.[146]

In 1865, Camp Return was established to quarter returning units as they waited to be mustered out and paid. Described by veterans of the 57th Pennsylvania Infantry as "adjoining 'Old Camp Curtin,'" Camp Return's exact location remains unknown.[147] As of June 3, the 51st, 141st, 142nd, 200th, 205th and 207th through 210th Pennsylvania Infantry were quartered in the camp. Eighty-four men belonging to the 110th Pennsylvania were also situated there. The 50th Pennsylvania also found itself at Camp Return in late July. Additional troops almost certainly passed through Camp Return, but many (including men of the regiments listed here) more often than not still referred to the location as Camp Curtin. The possibility also arises that some references to Camp Return are actually of the "old" Camp Curtin. However, the description provided by the men of the 57th clearly states that Camp Return was "adjoining" Camp Curtin, implying separate camps.[148]

Chapter 3

Life in Camp Curtin

I have heard more nois[e] in the last 24 hours than you have heard in the last 5 years.[149]
—*Private Orrin Mortimer Stebbins, Camp Curtin, June 5, 1861*

When Captain Joseph Matchette of the 46th Pennsylvania was asked to describe his experience in Camp Curtin more than sixty years later at age eighty-one, he offered this humorous but nonetheless revealing reminiscence: "No hostess houses, no banquets, no dances, no free chocolate and no ice cream at Camp Curtin."[150] An estimated 300,000 soldiers were quartered in the camp at some time during their service. For many, their time in Camp Curtin on the old Dauphin County Agricultural Fairgrounds was their first initiation into soldiery as well as the horrid war that had engulfed the nation. Nearly every soldier who ever entered Camp Curtin's gates had a distinct memory of the camp and their tenure inside it, whether positive or negative.

As new volunteers arrived in Harrisburg, they often found an incredible amount of activity within the city, along with enticing offers. Edgar Walters, a volunteer who arrived in July 1864, later reminisced:

The streets were full of soldiers—officers and privates, some glittering in new and flashing uniforms, others, whose tattered "blues," and bronzed faces gave evidence that they had seen long and arduous service. The corners were placarded with huge bills, calling for volunteers, substitutes &

etc., each one extolling the merits of its particular officers, or company in glowing terms. A number of accommodating gents, in citizens clothing came up to us, and commenced in admirable and astonishing strains, to inform us of "huge bounties," "splendid officers" and similar advantages which they could obtain for us, but we cut their eloquent appeals short by abruptly leaving them, and travelling on, towards Camp Curtin, passing the State House on Capitol Hill with its huge dome on our way.[151]

The process of arriving in Camp Curtin typically differed little for the many regiments that passed through Harrisburg during the war. The regiment or company would usually arrive in the city via rail and then march north through the town on Ridge Road to Camp Curtin. The roughly one-mile-long trek out to Camp Curtin was often arduous and grueling for young recruits. "This tried the endurance of the 'delicate young infants' considerably for the first day's experience in soldiering," recalled one soldier in the 126th Pennsylvania. "One of the company, from whom the respiration was rolling profusely, drolly remarked 'if this continues much longer I am afraid I'll meet a watery grave.'"[152] In September 1862, then captain George McFarland described his nine-month company's arrival at Camp Simmons:

After vexatious delays at Mifflin and on the way, we arrived at Harrisburg Depot at half past two yesterday the [September] 27th. There we took our first meal of soldier fare consisting of coffee, Ham and good Bread, but without butter or other home delicacies. After this, we marched up to Camp, reported to Capt [William A.] Tarbutton, and after some grumbling, got our requisition for tents, blankets, Kettles and other Camp equipage. These are received except the tents. Of these there was no supply on hand, and we were supplied with nothing but a "Markee [sic]," But through the kindness of some of Capt. Robinson's men (Juniata Cavalry encamped a few squares from us) the prospects of a rainy night without tents were dispelled, and by nine o'clock at night we had up 2…Markee's and 3 Common tents, ready for occupancy, though without straw or boards to keep us out of the great quantities of dust on the ground…which was converted into mud by the rains of the night. Tired and weary, after a poor supper of our own Cooking, we lay down; but the novelty of our position and the quality of our beds kept most of our men from sleep… The morning dawned very inauspiciously, for rain[,] mud and a chilly atmosphere prevailed. But in an hour or two, the weather cleared up, and what seemed very unfavorable, proved exactly the contrary; for the sandy soil of our camp soon absorbed the rain that had fallen, and we were relieved of the dust that formerly annoyed us. Breakfast tasted very agreeable, though it was late, and consisted of nothing but hard crackers, fired beef and pork, and Coffee.[153]

At Camp Curtin, thousands of soldiers-to-be received their first initiation into the life of a soldier. Often an unpleasant introduction, many men later linked their recollections of this distasteful experience to where it occurred: Camp Curtin. "I have no pleasant memories connected with my stay in Camp Curtin, and I have never heard any soldier who was there speak well of it," wrote Sergeant J.D. Bloodgood of the 141st Pennsylvania. "Coming as we did from pleasant homes to such a barren, dreary, uninviting spot, it is no wonder that the change was anything but agreeable."[154] "My first impression of camp life was anything but agreeable," Nicholas Rice, a corporal in the 50th Pennsylvania, concurred. "The great greasy black kittles strung on a pole over an open fire, and tended by a cook who much resembled the kettles, put a damper on my appetite. I could think of nothing but making soap in the spring time."[155] One soldier belonging to the 149th Pennsylvania was even harsher in his memory of the camp: "We had but two tents, and these the officers slept in—and we had to sleep in the open air that night," referring to his first night in Camp Curtin. "This we tho't was a good beginning of a soldier's life," he sarcastically remarked. "It was very warm all the time we were there; the air was so saturated with dust, and the offensive smell which attends the place we could hardly stand it." All he and his Clearfield, Pennsylvania comrades could think of was clean air: "We often wished for some…old Clearfield fresh air." The Clearfield boys departed Camp Curtin only ten days after their arrival, "and I can assure you that no one was sorry," he declared.[156]

Men of the "Doylestown Guards," later part of the 25th Pennsylvania, spent their first night in Camp Curtin under the cover of a Methodist camp meeting tent. "As the boys lay down in the clean straw to sleep off the fatigues of the day, 'with their martial cloaks around them,' they not only thought of the girls they had left behind them, but of their mothers' soft beds they had exchanged for the 'cold, cold ground,'" their captain, William W.H. Davis, later noted.[157] "We arrived in Camp Curtin the [August] 18th," penned Captain W.L. Lord of the 45th Pennsylvania, "and our first night in camp is still remembered. We had A tents and with half of a dirty army blanket lay on the ground without any other covering except our clothing. We had come out of feather beds at home and the contrast could be felt."[158]

Accounts of miserable first nights in Camp Curtin—which for many was also their first night experiencing the hardships of a soldier—are plentiful. As Eugene Beauge of the 45th Pennsylvania later wrote, although there was not "anything particularly remarkable" about his first night in Camp Curtin, "the experience was new and made a lasting impression." This lasting impression of a miserable and often wet evening served to kindle a negative memory of that night and the place where that night was spent. Lasting, negative memories are evident in Beauge's detailed description of his first night, recalled many years later: "It began to rain about dark and kept it up the greater part of the night. The quarters assigned to us were rickety, leaky old barracks, with nothing inside but the bare walls and the floor sopping wet with the rain that came down through the roof. Of course we had no bedding of any kind, not even a blanket that night. But as most of us had not slept a wink the night before and were 'all in' from the unusual excitement of the last few days, the boys were in good trim to sleep most anywhere and probably would have rested all right on the bare, wet floor if it hadn't been for the infernal racket of the cars that seemed to be in perpetual motion, the locomotive whistle getting busy every time we shut our eyes. The trouble was there were no railroads in those days in the neck of the woods where most of us came from and we were not used to that sort of thing." The general phraseology that Beauge uses in his account implies strong negative memory—"rickety, leaky old barracks" and the "infernal racket of the cars," for example.[159]

To Lyman Beebe of the 151st Pennsylvania, his experience in Camp Simmons in October 1862 was better than he had expected; however, the general atmosphere was unappealing to the forty-four-year-old farmer from Susquehanna County. "[I]t is the roughest place that a man ever was put in," he informed his mother. "[T]here is hollering and swearing all the time night and day." Beebe's letters lend important insight into the causes for displeasure among many soldiers in Camp Curtin. "I am doing first rate," he penned on October 22. "I am well and get enough to eat and they have given us more cloth[e]s than we know what do with." For Beebe, his distaste for life in Camp Simmons stemmed more from the unpleasant atmosphere of the camp—the "hollering and swearing"—than from camp conditions.[160]

Many arriving in Camp Curtin were simply awestruck at the sheer amount of men within the camp. For the majority of the rural, backcountry townspeople and farmers who arrived in Camp Curtin, it was the first time they were exposed to such large crowds, providing yet another reason for some soldiers' distaste for the encampment. "I have heard more nois[e] in the last 24 hours than you have heard in the last 5 years," penned Private Orrin Mortimer Stebbins in June 1861. "I saw one night this week over 30000 soldiers, and more than 10000 spectators in one mass. It was one scene of commotion."[161] "Camp Curtin was a lively place in those days," recalled Eugene Beauge of the 45th Pennsylvania. "It seemed to be full of young men, some strutting around with new uniforms on, others like ourselves in citizens clothes. In the forenoon especially everybody seemed to be doing something or going somewhere. Drilling by regiments, companies, and squads was going on all over the field." To Beauge, afternoons in Camp Curtin were "more quiet. Most of the men seemed to be taking it easy, lolling around or amusing themselves playing ball, checkers, cards or maybe writing letters."[162]

Typically, when soldiers first arrived in Camp Curtin, they received tents, silverware and dishware, as well as other various pieces of camp equipage. When Private Samuel North of the 126th Pennsylvania entered Camp Curtin, he and his comrades received "tents, kettles, frying pan to a mess, a tin place, spoon, knife and fork, [and] blanket." In most cases, shortly after receiving their equipage, men at Camp Curtin would be examined by surgeons to determine if they were physically fit for service. The normal procedure for examination included the men stripping bare, after which they would undergo a thorough examination by the physician on duty. "It was a strict examination," penned North. "We were stripped and brought out simply into an open tent in view of the whole company and we were felt and fingered all over." In an era marked by modesty, this exposure was particularly disconcerting for many men undergoing examination. "I would have given five dollars to have got clear," North noted.[163] Remarkably few men were turned away during this examination process—typically one or two men per company or, in some cases, none. Those who were passed by the examining surgeon were usually sworn in next and then received their uniforms.[164] "[T]hey consist of one over coat[,] one nice dress coat[,] one pair of pants[,] two pair drawers[,] two shirts[,] two pair socks[,] one pair shoes[,] knapsack and haversack[,] one ruber blanket [and] one wollen blanket," wrote Lyman Beebe from Camp Simmons. "[T]hey are all thick and heavy and it [is] a puzzle to us…what we green ones is going to do with them."[165]

Similar to virtually all other military encampments during the nineteenth century, life in Camp Curtin was accompanied by daily duties or chores. "Our duties in Camp Curtin were not strenuous enough to hurt anybody," reminisced Eugene Beauge, "although they kept us busy most of the time drilling, 'policing' the streets and standing guard." For Beauge and many of his comrades, drill "was an agreeable pastime at first. But when we had to practice the manual of arms with a gun weighing 15 pounds and go through manoeuvers with accoutrements on…well, we did it because we had to." "Cleaning or policing the streets was a sort of drudgery," admonished the Pennsylvanian, "but no one ever hurt himself doing it." Typically, a detail of several men from each company would be charged with sweeping and cleaning the grounds on a daily basis. Perhaps the most unpleasant assignment in the camp was guard duty. Guards were stationed along the perimeter of the camp, complemented by a line of pickets posted farther outside the premises with "instructions to overhaul all soldiers found outside without passes." Guards were often armed with only old muskets and wooden clubs. When Private Charles Brown of the 50th Pennsylvania was detailed for guard duty, he was armed with only "an old flintlock musket, all bent…just the barrel of the gun, and…a big club." "We did picket duty on the different roads leading from camp and at the gate, more to pick up stragglers found wandering around without a pass than anything else," admitted Beauge. Not only was it fairly simple for perpetrators to elude the detection of the guards and pickets, but those who were noticed might also escape a night in the lice-infested guardhouse with a well-spoken, passionate and convincing explanation.[166]

With a trained medical eye, Surgeon Alfred L. Castleman of the 5th Wisconsin was appalled by sanitary conditions at Camp Curtin. The unhealthy premises were perhaps the most frequent complaint about the encampment. "For months this had been a rendezvous for regiment after regiment," wrote Castleman, whose unit arrived at Camp Curtin in late July 1861. "The grounds had not been cleaned—the weather was intensely hot, without a leaf to intercept the scorching rays of the sun. The stench of the camp was intolerable, and the sickness of the troops rapidly increased." While at Camp Curtin, Castleman "made it my business to visit every tent twice a day, to see that they were thoroughly cleaned, and that the sides of the tent were raised so as freely to admit a current of air. But here the air was so foul as to improve the condition inside but little."[167]

Unfortunately for the health of the men in Camp Curtin, not all surgeons were as vigilant as Castleman. Opportunities for the spread of disease and illnesses were abundant in Camp Curtin. Volunteer Allen A. Van Orsdale, who had arrived in the camp shortly after its establishment, observed that all the men in his company suffered from "slight colds caused by mode of sleeping which is a blanket spread on the ground

Engraving of the Camp Curtin General Hospital. *Historical Society of Dauphin County.*

or straw and overcoats as pillows and a blanket as coverlid."[168] William Self, a volunteer from the small town of Osceola, Pennsylvania, situated near the New York–Pennsylvania border, detailed that after only a week in Camp Curtin, "we began to get dirty and sick and no liklyhood of a change." Six weeks into life at the camp, Self and his comrades were still living impoverished: "[I]t was rather tough for all of us but I have been here six weaks to day and no cloth[e]s but those which I wore away[—] shirt and a pair of pance which lasted about three weaks."[169]

Elaborating on Self's account, clothing was an ongoing problem throughout the war in Camp Curtin, especially during the winter months. "Most of the men had come to camp in their shirt sleeves, being led to believe that as soon as they should arrive in camp, army clothing would be issued to them," reported Captain Thomas Parker of the 51st Pennsylvania. The men of the 51st spent nearly half a month in camp during the fall of 1861 before they received any tolerable military garb. Shortly after their arrival, the Pennsylvanians were issued "a lot of old tattered blankets and bed quilts" that had seen service earlier that summer with the three-month troops raised in April 1861. The men of the 51st soon discovered the sheets were "alive with *vermin*," prompting the Pennsylvanians to toss the fabrics in their company streets and ignite the piles. Fortunately, the ladies of Harrisburg and the surrounding vicinity learned of their troubles and generously loaned the 51st "quilts sufficient for its comfort until the government could supply it."[170]

Surgeon James L. Dunn of the 109th Pennsylvania, which was encamped at Camp Wilkins near Pittsburgh, journeyed to Harrisburg on business around the beginning of June 1861. "After breakfast I went out to Camp Curtin and saw how they fared," he wrote to his wife. "They are not as well off, and the men do not compare with the men in Camp Wilkins. As a general thing the men look green and young. Our great, strong heavy-whiskered fellows are impressive compared to the greenhorn soldiers in Curtin."[171] Dunn believed that sanitary troubles in Camp Curtin were due to the quality of soldiers within, which may have been part of the trouble. Captain Parker of the 51st Pennsylvania later detailed that the

> health of the regiment was not good while at this camp, the men being too "green and raw" to stand the exposure at first; and the change from sleeping in comfortable feather beds and dry rooms to lying upon the damp ground or hard boards, with but scanty covering, was too sudden and severe for the human constitution to bear…the enlisted men…suffered extremely with diarrhoea, dysentery, and rheumatism. The change of food, no doubt, tended in a great measure to bring on the first two diseases, aided by the exposed condition of the comfortless sleeping quarters. Typhoid, camp, and other fevers began to seize the men towards the latter part of their stay in Camp Curtin.[172]

Although Dunn's concept has some credence, the camp's unsanitary conditions and atmosphere were certainly the main contributors to the unhealthiness of soldiers in Camp Curtin.

Another key facet of Camp Curtin's generally negative repute was the daily rations that were issued there. The fare at the camp was typically bearable but often not all too agreeable. "Our Camp fare is not extra but we can get along very well," penned one soldier in August 1862. "We get coffee, without cream, twice a day—Bread twice a day—Soup once and army crackers once a day." The "army crackers," commonly known as hardtack, were often dangerously stale. "An army cracker or army bread is very hard," described one volunteer, who decided to send a piece of his army cracker home, "just for you folks to see and bite into." However, he warned, "bite steady as there is great danger of breaking teeth."[173]

Religion was an important part of life for most soldiers in Camp Curtin. Nearly every regiment had its own chaplain, who held services regularly, and on infrequent occasions, companies in camp were afforded the opportunity to march to Harrisburg and attend church services. However, more often than not, religious services were held in a hodgepodge fashion within the camp limits. "It was a beautiful sight to see each company form in the lanes of their tents and then march out, forming a hollow square—less one side," described a correspondent for the *Pittsburgh Dispatch*, who witnessed the 11th Pennsylvania Infantry's Sunday services in November 1861. "The pulpit consisted of a dry goods box, with an upright board nailed on, and a rest on the top for a Bible, a blanket thrown over the whole, making quite a respectable pulpit." The Sabbath was not entirely reserved for religious practices and, save a brief service, often resembled a weekday. "Sunday…is the same here as any other day," opined one soldier. "Cars running, drums beating, fifes playing, soldiers drilling."[174] During the summer of 1863, the U.S. Christian Commission made a number of improvements about the camp, namely making religious services more accessible to soldiers quartered there. The commission established a "large tent upon the camp ground, capable of holding over a thousand men," where divine service was held every afternoon and evening. "Every soldier is supplied at this tent with a testament," detailed a Pennsylvania militiaman stationed at the camp that summer, "together with what other religious matter he wishes…They also have erected in one end of the tent, tables to accommodate fifty men at once, with seats, pens, ink, paper and envelopes, all free, so that none may have an excuse for not writing to their friends. They have a post office, and take to, and bring from, the city office, all soldiers' letters who request it. Altogether the Commission is doing a good deal for the comfort and good of the soldiers."[175]

"The soldiers in camp are not without their fun," reported the *Patriot* just days after the camp's founding. "Such a congregation contains all the different orders of men." Even less than a week after Camp Curtin's establishment, editors from the *Patriot* who visited the camp found that "[n]early all the tents have charcoal sketches upon them." Among the more noteworthy inscriptions the *Patriot* correspondents found was one tent christened "Fort Pickens," after the Yankee fortress located in Florida, and another one more humorously titled "Lazy Club." One tent even bore a life-size caricature of Confederate president Jefferson Davis.[176] More than a year later, apparently little had changed in this respect. In August 1862, a correspondent for the *Philadelphia Press* visited Camp Curtin and described his observations of the tents and camp life: "[W]e proceeded down the long row of tents and took a survey of their occupants. In one tent, marked 'Wyoming Tigers,' (by the way, all the tents have names given them), was a party of volunteers striking up the pathetic ba'lad of 'The Girl I left behind me;' in another the occupants were busily engaged writing letters to loved ones far away; a little farther on was a stout son of the old Keystone delivering the martial speech of 'King Henry before the walls of Harfleur' to a crowd of admiring friends."[177]

In another instance during Camp Curtin's early days, soldiers took to the art of parody. Several pranksters convinced a soldier to impersonate Confederate general Pierre G.T. Beauregard, made famous from his prominent role in the opening shots of the war at Fort Sumter. Tying the imposter to a rail, which was hoisted on the shoulders of four men, the faux Southern general was marched around the camp while a large assemblage of more than a thousand men followed, chanting and hurrahing "with all their might." "[T]he next performance was to kill and bury them which they did in real mock style and then dispersed for the night," reported one witness.[178] Sports and various games were also not lost to the soldiers quartered in the camp. "In the evenings after dress parade, a large number of the boys would congregate on the drill-ground for various amusements," later wrote one Pennsylvanian, "such as 'corner or baseball,' wrestling, running, jumping, and tossing up each other in blankets."[179]

Undoubtedly among Camp Curtin's most serious flaws was the lax discipline frequently exercised there. "Discipline was not very rigid in camp," later recalled Private Francis M. Smith of the 207th Pennsylvania.[180] Although some new recruits thought what little enforcement there was offered harsh and unreasonable, compared to most other military establishments in use throughout the war, Camp Curtin was rather unruly. For the majority of the camp's existence, passage in or out of the premises was fairly simple for soldiers and civilians alike. It was not uncommon for "a vast concourse of visitors from the city" to attend ceremonies in camp such as flag presentations.[181] Orders dictated that soldiers would remain in camp unless they had a pass, and civilians likewise would not be permitted to enter without a pass. However, obtaining the sought-after pass was relatively uncomplicated, and more often than not, curious civilians as well as peddlers and sutlers who had profit in mind were able to enter and exit practically at their own will. Some of the more clever soldiers within the encampment even invented a system of bogus passes that went undetected, enabling them access to the city's bountiful supplies of goods, foods and alcohol.[182]

For soldiers within the camp, desertion or simply leaving the camp without a pass was a fairly simple task. Edgar Walters of the 195th Pennsylvania later reminisced about the ease of leaving Camp Curtin: "[A]s there was not a very strict guard, we occasionally walked into town." "We all went to Harrisburg in our citizen clothes," recalled Henry F. Charles of the 172nd Pennsylvania Drafted Militia. "If a man wanted to leave all he had to do was put his uniform on over his citizen clothes. When he would get outside [of Camp Curtin] he would get behind a stretch of fence that was handy, strip off the blues throw them away and be on his way in his citizen outfit. Some times you could pick up 20 to 60 blue suits along [the] back of a fence." Charles himself journeyed home three times without leave.[183] However, when the city was placed under martial law on several occasions—most notably during the Maryland Campaign in mid-September 1862 and the Gettysburg Campaign in June and July 1863—regulations tightened significantly. No one, soldier or citizen, could travel in or out of Harrisburg without a provost marshal's pass. After 9:00 p.m., Provost Guard patrols would arrest any man without a pass or satisfactory excuse. Any citizens strolling through the streets past that hour would be taken to their home and, if not identified there, would be arrested for fear that the accused was a Southern spy.[184]

Throughout the war, the symbol of what little discipline there was in Camp Curtin remained the guardhouse in the southeastern corner of the camp. A night in Camp Curtin's guardhouse typically meant having to put up "with some drunken rowdies and deserters," who abounded the structure virtually every night. Additionally, reports of abundant lice in the building struck fear into thousands of soldiers. Detainees inside the guardhouse were fed dry bread and water. Several corporals were assigned the unpleasant task of transporting the prisoners from the guardhouse to the privy, where they were to "wait on him till he is done, and then bring him back to the guard-house."[185] Further punishment awaited those who misbehaved in the guardhouse. Eli Strouss of the 57th Pennsylvania noted that "[t]here is plenty of fun here sometimes. If a fellow gets drunk here they put him in the Guard house and [if] he does not behave there they make him ride the cannon. It looks funny to see a fellow a straddle of a cannon tied so he cannot get off. A fellow rode it last week, all night and it rained like fury all the time."[186] By the fall of 1861, the cannon had become a part of daily life in Camp Curtin. Often known as "the big cannon," it was situated in front of the camp headquarters at Floral Hall. The piece was fired every morning at 6:00 a.m., notifying men encamped on the premises to awaken for roll call, and then every evening at 9:00 p.m., signaling soldiers to begin their slumber.[187]

Yet another reason life in Camp Curtin proved difficult was due to the exorbitant prices often charged for necessary articles. Purchasing paper, envelopes and stamps was costly before and even after the Christian Commission made writing materials available to soldiers during the summer of 1863. In an unpatriotic manner, many Harrisburg merchants raised prices on items they knew would be in demand. Corporal Lyman Beebe of the 151st Pennsylvania, who was quartered in Camp Simmons, wrote in November 1862:

> It is the hardest kind of a place for a man to live in here, for there is many things that we have to buy, and we have to pay three times as much as they are worth. [T]obacco is 75 cents a pound[,] washing is 6 cents a peese for shirts[,] drawers and socks. 10 cents a peese for puting in pockets[,] 18¾ cents for sewing on the strips on our coat sleeves. 45 cents for shoe brush[,] 10 cents for box of black[en]ing. [T]hey require us to keep our boots blacked. [A]ll these things counts up rather fast.[188]

Numerous soldiers found it difficult to live without many of these necessities. "I want some money to pay my postage and tobacco," penned Luther Granger of the 57th Pennsylvania, who found himself in Camp Curtin in November 1861. "[T]hey are very useful articles so much so that I cannot do without a little to get along with times."[189]

Another frequent complaint about life in Camp Curtin was the climate. When the rain came down heavy, tents often flooded. In September 1861, the men of Captain George Pechin's Montgomery County company were forced to abandon their tents "to avoid being submerged by the 'sea of rushing waters'" as the rain "poured down in torrents."[190] In addition to rain, passing winters in Camp Curtin was difficult. Luther Granger of the 57th Pennsylvania likened conditions in Camp Curtin during the winter of 1861 to being "cold enough to freeze a dog." The frigid winter weather made life particularly miserable for those detailed on guard duty. When Granger was called on for guard duty at the guardhouse, he spent an unpleasant few hours of the evening shivering in the cold. "I am sure although I had as warm a place as could be had," noted Granger, "but yet I was cold."[191]

On the opposite end of the spectrum, summers at Camp Curtin were often rendered similarly unpleasant. "[I]t seems that the weather was never so hot, the dust never so deep, and shade trees never so scarce as at present," recorded a soldier in the 6th Pennsylvania Reserves. "We cannot exercise out-of-doors in the heat of the day, and when it is cool we have plenty of drilling to do and frequently when it is not so cool. Tents, in very hot weather, are anything but comfortable, and if we can only get under the shade of a board, we have not the ambition to be anything but satisfied."[192] On a similar note, Chaplain David Craft of the 141st Pennsylvania later wrote, "The constant tread of thousands of feet had…not only destroyed every vestige of grass, but had ground the surface into dust which every puff of wind sent in clouds across the encampment. This with the pelting heat of an August sun and a prevailing drought, made that almost treeless plain seem cheerless as a desert."[193] Just as difficult to deal with as the inclement climate was the dust continually clogging the atmosphere—a frequent complaint. This was a problem only complicated by the massive presence of troops constantly drilling and marching, in the process further stirring up the dust. "I will be very glad to go as it is so very dusty here," complained one soldier. "Clouds of dust are in the atmosphere constantly." "Camp Curtin (on as windy a day as this) is one of the dirties and dustiest places Ive ever Been," wrote Sergeant Jacob Zorn. "[T]heres no end to dust."[194]

For both enlisted men and officers, one of the most irritating and unruly parts of life in Camp Curtin was being mustered out at the premises. Often the process of finalizing the muster rolls was lackluster at best, and enlisted men tantalized at the prospect of returning home often grew irritated toward their officers. In the 200th Pennsylvania, after several days of anxiously awaiting to be paid and mustered out, Adjutant's Clerk Jonathan W. Kerr could clearly discern that the enlisted men in his regiment were "becoming impatient." The following day, matters worsened. "The boys throughout the Regt began to sprout ugly and be very noisy," Kerr recorded. The men ridiculed several officers "awfully," and some fighting broke out among the ranks.[195] Often mustering officers were the cause of this delay. During the summer of 1863, the muster out of one Pennsylvania militia regiment was delayed several days because the mustering officer, Captain Joseph Bush of the 13th U.S. Infantry, was "more fond of carousing about the hotels of Harrisburg than attending to his business."[196] In August 1865, as the 16th Pennsylvania Cavalry returned to Harrisburg to be mustered out, Adjutant Samuel Cormany noted that at "old Camp Curtin…[a] motley crowd looked us over—agents and bad women played their arts on unwary men in the camp." Four days later, with the regiment still in Camp Curtin, Cormany noted that "[a]ll too many are drinking and being disorderly—But they are now Citazens, and our official control is nil." Cormany remarked that although military protocol "still counts somewhat as mild restraint," the "whiskey blunts respect…and one is measurably helpless."[197]

Archives abound with letters from Camp Curtin complaining about camp conditions, exorbitant prices and tedious drills. While these documents represent the overwhelming majority of soldiers who passed through Camp Curtin, the opinions expressed do not hold true for each and every soldier who spent time in the camp. Remarkably enough, a number of men managed to embrace and enjoy their stay in the encampment. Shortly after his enlistment, Eli C. Strouss of the 57th Pennsylvania arrived at Camp Curtin in October 1861. "I like it first rate so far and I never felt better in my life," Strouss informed a friend. "If I would never fare worse than I do now I would be in camp for life all the time." Strouss is the epitome of an optimist. "We drill about 10 hours a day [w]hich is first rate exercise," he penned.[198]

Much like life for the enlisted men in Camp Curtin, the daily duties of Camp Curtin's commandant were typically monotonous and often unpleasant. The commandant was charged with overseeing that troops were mustered in, maintaining discipline and order and authorizing requisitions, among other things. More often than not, commandants were appointed from regiments currently in the camp. Typically, these officers served as commandant for less than a month and turned over their duties when their regiment departed the camp. For instance, the first officer to serve in this role at Camp Curtin, Lieutenant Colonel Washington H.R. Hangen of the 9th Pennsylvania, remained in his post for roughly two weeks, until his regiment departed the camp.

Perhaps the best account of the daily life and responsibilities of Camp Curtin's commandant is left by Lieutenant Colonel Alfred B. McCalmont. Lieutenant colonel of the 142nd Pennsylvania, McCalmont was ordered on recruiting duty in mid-March 1864. When he initially arrived in Harrisburg on April 3, his future there was uncertain. Six days later, however, McCalmont received an order from the War Department detailing him as commandant of Camp Curtin. Early on, he seemed discontent with his position and eager to depart for elsewhere. "I am still here without any intimation of orders to leave," the lieutenant colonel penned on May 13, "though it is possible the camp will be vacated ere long. It seems to be diminishing in importance." After one month in this new role, his daily life had essentially been confined to authorizing requisitions, visiting his family in Harrisburg and listening intently to news from the front. By his May 13 letter, McCalmont had received news of the bloody engagements between Lee and Grant in the Wilderness, in which his regiment suffered heavily. "I am satisfied that I escaped the terrible trial," McCalmont informed his brother. "It is true it would have been more creditable to have been with my men, but when I sat down to tea this evening with my wife and children I had no regret for the lost honor."

The Venango County native openly admitted his opinion that he was "of no use" at Camp Curtin. However, he also realized that his regiment "is not now larger than a full company, and I cannot see that I would be of any more service in front." Therefore, McCalmont decided that he would "not make any effort either to remain or to be ordered to the front, but shall obey orders." The monotony of his position quickly turned hectic and eventful on June 6, when the famed Pennsylvania Reserve Corps arrived in the city to be mustered out. The lieutenant colonel soon realized that serious work lay ahead of him. After their memorable reception in the city, the reserves filed north of town to Camp Curtin. Several days later, most of the reserves still remained in camp, waiting to be mustered out. "They had great difficulty in making out their rolls," McCalmont recorded. Further crowding the camp were other returning three-year regiments. "There are eight more regiments of Pennsylvania Volunteers to be discharged this month [June 1864]," he admonished, "and five or six in July." One month earlier, McCalmont had pondered when Camp Curtin would be closed. Now, as the camp grew more congested by the day, he prepared to remain for the rest of the summer. "My camp will therefore probably not be broken up, and I may remain here a month longer."[199]

"I have had enough to do during the last few days," penned the Venango County officer on July 20. "I have hardly had time to eat." McCalmont's troubles with mustering out the reserves and other three-year regiments were compounded when President Lincoln called for volunteers to serve one hundred days in response to Confederate general Jubal Early's northern thrust into Maryland during the first days of July 1864. Pennsylvania formed six regiments (192nd through 197th Pennsylvania Volunteers), several of which were mustered in at Camp Curtin. "We have about two thousand one hundred days' men in camp and they are still arriving," estimated McCalmont. With the influx of men coming into Camp Curtin, Commandant McCalmont proved a rigid disciplinarian. Perhaps his harshest measure was to exclude women from the camp. "It was found that under pretense of selling pies and doing washing, they stole large quantities of blankets, tents and other property, and that they carried on prostitution to an extent that would seem incredible," he confided. "They used to come up in droves."

McCalmont's hectic schedule also prevented him from spending time in Harrisburg and with his family. "I have not been in town often for a week," he detailed. The peace and quiet McCalmont sought was certainly not available at camp headquarters in Floral Hall. "At night Oliver and I have the building to ourselves, but business commences at daylight and then there is nothing but a rush till after dark," McCalmont wrote. "We have twenty companies of one hundred men in camp. They are to be sent to Washington to-morrow evening. I am sitting up late to sign requisitions whenever wanted," the commandant grumbled. "They do not give me time to eat."

Volunteers soon began arriving in camp to serve a term of one year. McCalmont was further bombarded with offers from these new volunteers to serve as their colonel. "Some of the officers wish me to take the Colonelcy of one of them, but I am not quite satisfied to do it," he wrote. "It is the only way I can get promotion, but I do not know that it would be in other respects of any advantage. I would be in a brigade commanded by some man who has seen less service than myself, which was one of the evils incident to the life in Virginia. Then the idea of leaving my wife and children in a week for another winter campaign is not agreeable." However, one week later, McCalmont accepted the colonelcy of the 208th Pennsylvania. Although he was detained until November to complete his duties as camp commandant, McCalmont would join the 208th in the field in November and serve in a number of engagements near Richmond, notably during the Siege of Petersburg.[200]

Overall, it is clear that there was a strongly negative stigma forever bound to Camp Curtin in the memories of most of the soldiers who were quartered there. Although unsanitary conditions, often strict and exacting daily routines and the delays so often in occurrence certainly played a role in the camp's undesirable reputation, there were other factors at play. For many exuberant volunteers eager to take the field, Camp Curtin was the one and only obstacle between them and active field service. This group of men found the time spent at Camp Curtin disagreeable not just because of its disease-filled premises but also because of the days, weeks and even months of their enlistment spent in tedious, monotonous drill at Camp Curtin; it was these men's belief that they should take to the field immediately. Reflecting on Camp Curtin, Chaplain David Craft of the 141st Pennsylvania noted that the "inactivity and restraints to which they were subject, the feeling that they were doing nothing toward the accomplishment of the object for which they had left their homes, made them restive and uneasy."[201] For the majority of soldiers, the time they spent in Camp Curtin was their transition from civilian life to army life, to which many had difficulty adjusting. "I at once began to adjust myself to the new mode of life so suddenly thrust upon me," recalled Private Henry F. Long of Company I, 17th Pennsylvania Cavalry, who was quartered in Camp Simmons. "I now realized that I had left home and friends, cut loose from civic life and joined the army. That I was no longer privileged to do as I pleased, but had to obey the orders of my superiors, right or wrong."[202]

Also noteworthy—and a fitting conclusion to this chapter—is the repeated use by many returning soldiers of the phrase "old Camp Curtin" during the latter stages of the war. Depending on how one interprets the expression, one could detect a subtle hint of affection or compassion for the camp—similar to that expressed for the "old Camelback bridge." For the thousands of soldiers who were first quartered within Camp Curtin, virtually every one carried with him for the remainder of his life some distinct memory of his initiation into soldiery there. Unpleasant or not, memories were created there, and perhaps this resulted in some faint affection for the old campground.

Chapter 4

Civilian-Soldier Interaction in Harrisburg

The boys never stole anything but the[y] *would draw about anything not nailed down, & even might draw the nails if it seemed worth while.*[203]
—Private Francis M. Smith, 207th Pennsylvania

The town of Gettysburg hosted two great armies during the summer of 1863. The community of Sharpsburg, Maryland, and the entire area surrounding Antietam Creek endured the bloodiest single day in American history, as well as its atrocious aftermath. The city of Harrisburg, on the other hand, never underwent a battle, although during the summer of 1863, the Confederate army neared within several miles of the Susquehanna. For more than four years nonstop, the Pennsylvania capital served as a continuous training and facilitation site for thousands of Northern soldiers on their way to the front lines. Only a few, select Northern cities have such a claim.

For a city that had such a lengthy and continuous association with the Northern war effort, and more specifically the rank and file who fueled it, an intriguing relationship between the citizenry and the military naturally formed. Understandably, this connection was frequently strained. There are many different conflicts and elements within this relationship between the citizens of Harrisburg and the military that was quartered within and around the city. From early on, struggles arose as nearby farmers accused soldiers of stealing crops and other eatables, as well as destroying property. In one instance during the fall of 1862, a fed-up farmer shot a soldier "who was engaged in the wanton destruction of his property." Reports frequented Harrisburg papers of theft and destruction of property, but more often than not, the mischief by soldiers in Harrisburg area camps was limited to food swindling.

Around Camp Curtin, some troublesome men from the camp had torn down the fences of various nearby farms, as well as fences that enclosed the stockyards of the Pennsylvania Railroad company, using the dismantled wooden rails for firewood. Near Camp McClellan, some distance north of Camps Curtin and Simmons, the cavalrymen quartered there snatched turkeys and chickens from farmers' pens, fruit from their orchards and, like the mischievous soldiers at Camp Curtin, fence rails for firewood. All sorts of "moveable property" disappeared every night. By November 1862, most Harrisburgers had had enough of the thievery and pilfering. It had proceeded on a consistent basis for more than a year, and that was unacceptable. Further outraging many Harrisburgers were rare cases—often questionable in accuracy but nonetheless popularized in city newspapers—of dangerous encounters between thieving soldiers and protesting civilians, where the former threatened "blows and death" when confronted.

True or not, these rumors incensed the people of Harrisburg. "Our farmers cannot stand these losses," exclaimed the editors of the *Telegraph*, which had received its share of complaints from local farmers. "They have all given freely and liberally to promote the comfort and ensure the contentment of the soldier, and therefore they should be protected from this vandalism by those in charge of the camps, or they may be driven to their own protection."[204] The general reaction among the citizens of Harrisburg to these claims throughout the fall of 1862 appears to have been a more hostile attitude toward pillaging soldiers. Civilians seemingly became more aggressive in their response to thefts by soldiers. In some ways, the condemning reports throughout late 1862 served as a tipping point in this part of the relationship between Harrisburgers and the military. Frustrated civilians no longer looked the other way at dishonorable acts by their nation's defenders. Interactions grew increasingly confrontational.

Considering the apparent ease soldiers experienced in entering and exiting Camp Curtin, it is not all that surprising that so many depredations on local farms occurred. At many times during the war, several thousand men were quartered within the camp; taking into account those who were legally passed out of camp combined with the clever soldiers who managed to leave the premises without permission, a large number typically roamed the streets and surrounding fields. The destruction that Harrisburg area farms received during the four years of war was not unheard of, especially in the

Southern states, where Yankee soldiers infamously pillaged civilian homes, fields and plantations. Perhaps what surprised Harrisburgers more was the fact that *Northern* soldiers were looting and wreaking havoc on *Northern* farms.

Predictably, complaints typically increased during times when Camp Curtin's population had increased on account of newly arriving troops. One instance of this pattern came during the fall of 1862. The influx of nine-month soldiers, drafted soldiers and the three-year cavalry regiments spiked Camp Curtin's population to unprecedented highs—leading to the creation of Camps Simmons and McClellan—and the threat of Confederate invasion in September 1862 brought additional troops to the city. Another notable example of this trend occurred during the summer of 1863, when thousands of Pennsylvania and New York militia occupied Harrisburg's west shore. With many families having abandoned their homes fearful of the approaching Confederates, the Yankee militiamen completely ransacked numerous houses and farms opposite Harrisburg.

For those soldiers who had been raised on strict moral values, within Camp Curtin they soon noticed the excuses by which their fellow comrades justified their often unruly behavior. Private Francis Smith of the 207th Pennsylvania, which was quartered in Camp Curtin during the fall of 1864, later recalled, "One morning I walked down to the company's cooking establishment & saw several large pails filled with fine potatoes, evidently fresh dug[.] 'Where did you get these?' I asked in some surprise of the cooks[.] 'Drew them' was the laconic reply." As Smith explained, "in the army we drew everything, so this sounded O.K." To Smith and many other young soldiers, they were introduced into a culture where "drawing" rations was standard and not a villainous act. Some of the more keen recruits, such as Smith, were curious exactly how the articles (or, in Smith's case, potatoes) were "drawn." Smith continued, "'But How?' I asked, 'By the tops,' & that was all I could learn, but I fancied that some farmer would be lamenting the loss of some bushels of good potatoes."

"The boys never stole anything," Smith later penned, "but the[y] would draw about anything not nailed down, & even might draw the nails if it seemed worth while…The boys liked cherries, & thot that while obeying their countrys call, they should have a share of the cherries, so the farmers & their families were kept busy defending their fruit." For those soldiers who were in Camp Curtin during Smith's time—in late 1864—the increased aggressiveness of area farmers served as an added difficulty in their quest for delectables from nearby farms. It was well known within Camp Curtin during Smith's time that farmers were prepared to defend their property, so much so that men inside the camp even devised a tactical strategy with which to wreak havoc on local farms. "A favorite plan of the boys was a flank attack, a real army maneuver," explained Smith. "While one party made a feint, a pretended attack on the front & kept the defenders busy at that point, the other would st[e]al around & attack the rear, so they would generally get a fair meal." Within his reminiscences, Smith recorded a good example of the increased aggressiveness not only among farmers but also their wives. One afternoon, a soldier made a particularly noticeable ruckus as he came sprinting into camp; this particular soldier had been "in the rear attack" but was "so busy" devouring his prize that the farmer's wife was able to "put in 2 or 3 good whacks with a pole before he could get out of the tree & make good his retreat."[205]

Perhaps Harrisburg civilians and the soldiers quartered about the city were never closer than during the fall of 1862 and the summer of 1863, the periods immediately following the Battles of Antietam and Gettysburg respectively. The massive casualties of these two battles were distributed across various Northern cities for care, Harrisburg included. No delusions were ever entertained that the Camp Curtin General Hospital, which reportedly contained ninety-four beds supplemented by additional hospital tents, could receive and care for the thousands of incoming men, so makeshift hospitals were opened across the city.[206] Not only were wounded Yankee soldiers to be cared for, but a large number of wounded Confederate prisoners of war also necessitated medical attention. Shortly after Antietam, the Cotton Mill was opened as a hospital to quarter the excess wounded. Due to both a shortage of cotton and a spike in the cost of the material, the mill had temporarily suspended operations during the summer of 1861 and a year later still remained idle. "Here we were very comfortable," recalled Henry Gerrish, a soldier quartered in the mill. When more room was needed, the proprietors of the factory opened "the long building in the rear of the factory" to accommodate more soldiers.[207]

Fears of a large battle near Harrisburg during the Gettysburg Campaign prompted the reopening of five additional hospitals during the last week of June 1863, many of which had seen use during the previous fall and winter. The city opened the Lancastrian schoolhouse at the corner of Walnut and Aberdeen Streets—later the site of the Technical High School and the Old City Hall—for use as a hospital, and the location soon became known as the East Walnut Street Hospital. By July 1, 1863, the schoolhouse-turned-infirmary was considered the "most extensive hospital" within the city.[208]

Harrisburg Cotton Mill, circa 1890. In 1888, the facility was converted to a silk mill until the 1920s, when the structure was demolished and replaced by the Young Men's Christian Association (YMCA). *Historical Society of Dauphin County.*

In late August 1863, editors from the *Patriot* toured the structure and later described their visit:

> *We enjoyed the privilege of a stroll through this hospital on Saturday evening, and passed an hour or two of pleasant intercourse with the Surgeon and some of the patients under his charge. From the former we learn that he now prescribes for 95 patients, of whom 54 are Unionists and 41 rebels. Of these latter, 3 are captains, 2 first lieutenants, 4 second lieutenants and 2 sergeants, representing all the Southern States except Texas and South Carolina. They fell into our hands at Gettysburg. Those officers with whom we conversed were men of scholastic attainments and affable and gentlemanly manners. There is perhaps no building in this vicinity, not built expressly for a hospital, which answers that purpose as well as the East Walnut institution. Being erected for a high school, it is large and commodious, and is divided into wards of the proper size on both floors. It now contains 146 beds, of which 20 are in tents outside the main building.*

*The whole is in charge of Surgeon R.H. Seiler and 2 assistants, with an
auxiliary force of 12 nurses and 19 guards.*[209]

In late September, the patients at the East Walnut Street Hospital were
transferred to other hospitals within the city, allowing the male students of
the Lancastrian school to return to their schoolhouse in early October.[210] The
West Walnut Street Hospital was established in an all-female schoolhouse at
the corner of Walnut Street and River Alley. A male schoolhouse located
"on Mulberry Street, near front," also cared for the wounded and was soon
popularized as the Mulberry Street Hospital; the Harrisburg Hospital was
later constructed on the site in 1873.[211] The German Reformed Church at
the corner of Third and Chestnut Streets opened its Sunday school room as
a temporary hospital during the fall of 1862, and the location soon came to
be dubbed the Chestnut Street Hospital.[212]

The Ladies' Union Relief Association of Harrisburg made it its priority
to visit the various hospitals about the city and provide care, comfort and
food to the wounded and sick soldiers. "Too much praise cannot be given
the ladies of Harrisburg, for the kindness and generosity which they have
shown the sick and wounded soldiers," penned one Pennsylvania militiaman
who was about the city during the summer of 1863. "I have visited four
large hospitals in the City, all filled with sick and wounded soldiers. Each
hospital is daily visited by a committee of ladies who furnish food for that
day. The wants of each soldier are carefully inquired of and kindly and
bountifully ministered to. Scores of ladies make it a daily business to visit the
hospitals, with kind, smiling faces, and hands filled with good things for the
sick soldier."[213]

One of the darker chapters of the relationship between Harrisburg
civilians and the men quartered in Camp Curtin occurred in August 1862.
On Friday, August 15, several soldiers reportedly died after eating poisoned
pies sold to them in the camp. "A very serious transaction took place in camp
on Friday," penned one soldier. "An old 'Secesh Wooman' came to camp with
poisoned pies and sold them to the soldiers and of course they died. Seven
died from the effects of them. She was arrested and is now, accordingly, in
prison. Those that died were pretty nearly all from Tioga County. Pie selling
is stopped in camp. All the rest of the peddlers were immediately kicked
out of camp."[214] News of the alleged deaths spread like wildfire throughout
the camp and city alike. J.P. Wilson, post surgeon at Camp Curtin, issued a
statement in response:

Reports having been circulated to the effect that several men had been poised at Camp Curtin by eating pies, containing strychnine, and that they had died from its effects. I deem it only just to state, that there is no foundation in fact or circumstance for this rumor. There has not been a single death in camp, or any sickness but a few mild cases of cholera morbus, caused by eating unripe fruit or vegetables, since the gathering of the recruits now in camp.[215]

Despite Wilson's solid rebuttal, more cases of alleged poisoning soon began to appear over the following days. "The camp is full of excitement at present, in consequence of the poisoning of four men this morning by eating apples, bought of apple women," recorded another soldier.[216] When a correspondent from the *Philadelphia Press* visited the camp on August 16—one day after the first alleged incident involving poisoned pies—he met soldiers who told him a variety of tales: "Some of the soldiers on the camp ground informed us that sixty men were poisoned by eating pies which they bought from a woman who was selling them on the ground, and another positively stated that he had cut an apple in two parts and found a large lump of strychnine in it." The *Press* correspondent interviewed Surgeon Wilson, who pronounced "the statement as a wicked fabrication, and informed us that the camp was unusually healthy, and that there had not been a single death in camp, or any sickness."[217] The evidence available suggests that the reported poisonings were more fiction than reality. Perhaps several questionable pies were consumed and that sparked the untamable rumor, but the reports of multiple deaths are entirely unfounded.

Reports of men in the camp being poisoned were nothing new; in fact, similar cases date back to the camp's first days. Less than a week after Camp Curtin was founded, sales to soldiers were limited "by reason of some reports…of the poisoning of several soldiers by eating cakes, &c., purchased from them [peddlers]." Further cause for alarm came in late April 1861 when large numbers of fish in the city reservoir were found dead, supposedly having been poisoned. Fearing what could happen if the reservoir were sabotaged, a guard was posted there night and day to ensure the safety of the city's water supply.[218]

Chapter 5

Copperhead Capital

The Politics of Civil War Harrisburg

I finally dozed and dreamed a little, with the shouts of the Copperheads ringing in my ears.[219]
—*Samuel Pennypacker, Pennsylvania militiaman, June 1863*

During the Civil War, Harrisburg served as an essential railroad hub, a major point for troop concentration and a training and facilitation center, among other things, but the city was still the state capital. Throughout the Civil War, Northern political parties were battling for control of governorships, state legislatures and city offices—races and conflicts that often polarized the city of Harrisburg. During the mid-nineteenth century, Harrisburg tended to lean Democratic. The city's first mayor, William H. Kepner, was a Democrat. Formerly president of the town council, Kepner was elected in 1860 and served through early 1863. However, by the time of Harrisburg's mayoral elections in March 1863, the incumbent Kepner found himself on the outs with his own party. The majority of Democrats wanted Kepner out of office because of the support he had given Lincoln and the Republican Party.

Kepner's Democratic challenger was "General" Augustus L. Roumfort, a native of Paris. After graduating from West Point in 1817, the Frenchman was appointed a second lieutenant in the navy but resigned after only eighteen months. He later became principal of the Military Academy at Mount Airy, near Philadelphia, served as the military storekeeper in Philadelphia during the administration of President Andrew Jackson, was a member of the state legislature and later became a brigadier general in the state militia. In 1850, Roumfort was selected as superintendent of the Eastern Division of the Pennsylvania Railroad, from which he retired in 1862. Throughout Harrisburg, he was known as "General Roumfort" on the grounds of his antebellum militia service. The extremist faction of the Democratic Party, which was largely backing Roumfort, were known as the "Copperheads." As the war progressed, the pro-Republican element of the Northern press coined the term "Copperheads" to refer derisively to any of a group of perceived Southern sympathizers, including Peace Democrats, certain ethnic and religious groups that appeared apathetic to the Southern war effort (particularly in the south-central tier of Pennsylvania) and others who openly vocalized opposition to the Lincoln administration's policies concerning the war. In the Democratic primary, held one week before the election, Mayor Kepner could only watch as Roumfort trounced him among his own party, carrying every ward in the city. An insurmountable wave of enthusiasm carried the Frenchman forward. Turnout at the primary was "much larger than has formerly characterized primary meetings of this kind in our city."[220]

Opposing Roumfort in the municipal election was John Till, a candidate for the Loyal League. A boat builder by trade, Till was determined to support and sustain the Northern war effort. Essentially the Republican ticket, the Loyal League's objectives included sustaining the war and aiding the government in any way necessary. Once again, Roumfort was triumphant, carrying four of the city's six wards, the exceptions being a tie in the Third Ward and a victory for Till in the Fifth Ward. Overall, the Frenchman counted 843 votes to Till's 785. The 1863 municipal election was a big triumph for the Democrats; the Democratic-leaning *Patriot* excitedly described it as the "Great Democratic Victory." The entire Democratic ticket was elected. Throngs of enthusiastic Democrats, or Copperheads, learned the results, fittingly, while gathered at the *Patriot and Union* office and journeyed to the Buehler House, where Mayor-elect Roumfort delivered a brief speech from the balcony due to popular demand.[221]

Also of interest are the various political interactions of the citizenry of Harrisburg. Unfortunately, contemporary accounts of political divisions from civilians themselves are lacking. However, the city's daily newspapers do lend important insight into the political polarization that the city underwent. On a daily basis, Harrisburg's two primary newspapers—the *Patriot* and the *Telegraph*—bickered at each other with malicious language and inflated accusations. Among the more frequently discussed topics were the Knights of the Golden Circle, a secret organization that infested south-central Pennsylvania, similar to the Copperheads in their sympathy for the Southern cause. The editors of the *Telegraph*—whose Republican lean was all but modest—blasted the group, often cautioning its readers to beware of its dangerous members. In October 1861, the newspaper printed a column on "How to Recognize a Knight of the Golden Circle." Several months later, the *Telegraph* claimed that the *Patriot* "had been sustained for months by means of contributions derived from the *Knights of the Golden Circle*" and even jokingly offered to publish the bylaws of the group if the editors of their rival paper would be kind enough to lend them their copy.[222]

Harrisburg also experienced its share of politics on the statewide level. The Keystone State's wartime governor was Andrew Gregg Curtin. Often known as the "soldier's friend," Curtin soon became identified as a strong ally of Lincoln's and one of the most devoted Northern war governors. These factors and many more drove a strong Democratic campaign to unseat him. During this effort, Harrisburg—and particularly the soldiers quartered within—experienced firsthand the malice of a heated gubernatorial campaign.

From all across the state, Democrats flocked to the capitol in Harrisburg, where the party's state convention—dubbed the "Copperhead Convention" by many—was held in the statehouse. Curtin was facing an uphill reelection fight in October 1863, and the Democrats were eager to nominate his opponent. That same month, June 1863, militia companies from across the state flocked to Harrisburg in response to calls from Governor Curtin to defend the city from Confederate invasion, and many who were not provided quarters wound up on the capitol grounds. This unpleasant reality came true for Samuel Pennypacker. In the summer of 1863, a soldier in a militia company from Phoenixville, Pennypacker was destined for future political stardom, later serving as governor of Pennsylvania. The future governor and his company arrived in Harrisburg via rail well into the evening of June 17. His spirits "somewhat chilled" by a lacking reception, after some deliberation Pennypacker and his comrades drifted toward the capitol grounds. "What before was uncertain and undefined became open indignation on reaching the Capitol buildings," he recalled.

The very night he arrived, the Democrats nominated Judge George Woodward—the associate judge and later chief justice of the Supreme Court of Pennsylvania—as their candidate to oppose Curtin for the governorship. "The Copperhead convention, which had assembled for the purpose of nominating a candidate for governor, had just chosen Judge Woodward, and held possession of the hall and seats of the House of

Governor Andrew Gregg Curtin. *Author's collection.*

Representatives, shouting, hurrahing and making inflammatory speeches, while the pavement, the stone porch, and the galleries were covered with militia, trying to sleep amidst the din," he described. Pennypacker and his fellow militiamen were incensed. "The thought was enough to anger a saint," he penned, "the Capital of the State threatened by the rebels, the Governor almost beseeching men to come to the rescue, and those who respond compelled to lie outside upon the stones and listen to the disloyal yells of the enemies of the country comfortably quartered within."

The original state capitol building, also known as the Hills Capitol after architect Stephen Hills, first opened in 1822 and was destroyed by fire in 1897. *Historical Society of Dauphin County.*

Young Samuel and two friends determined to attempt their slumber on the stone porch of the statehouse, which the trio deemed "the most eligible spot, being covered by a roof, more clean, cool and less crowded than the inside." Their opinion was confirmed when rain clouds (which others had neglected to notice) soon burst forth and soaked those less clever men who rested on the pavement. "I finally dozed and dreamed a little," Pennypacker wrote, "with the shouts of the Copperheads ringing in my ears." At about 1:00 a.m., the convention adjourned, and the Copperhead delegates "came stepping out over us, and went to their hotels, all of which they had previously engaged and crowded. The men groaned and cursed them," the future governor recorded, "d----d Woodward, McClellan, and traitors generally, and there were several fights in consequence."[223]

The pro-Republican editors of the *Telegraph* were enraged when reports reached them of maltreatment of soldiers by the Copperhead politicians and delegates they so despised. The paper reported a story that "a loyal, patriotic soldier, who had passed through the Mexican campaign, as well as the nine months' service, and who bears the scars of three honorable wounds received in the service of his country, took occasion to manifest his disapproval of the sentiment of the ignoble speaker by *hissing*." According to the *Telegraph*'s report, no sooner had the soldier sneered "than a general clamor of 'put him out,' 'kill him,' 'break his neck,' &c., resounded throughout the hall, and a score of copperheads rushed upon the poor fellow and ejected him from the place." In their defense of the soldier, the *Telegraph* could not help but also take a swipe at its rivals: "The soldier had but imitated the example of the copperheads…They [the copperheads] exercised the privilege of hissing, but are not willing that others should exercise it."[224]

Chapter 6

Harrisburg and the Gettysburg Campaign

*During this morning a perfect panic prevailed, extending to all classes
of people, and resulting in the grandest demand for railroad tickets ever
witnessed in this city.*[225]
–Philadelphia Daily Evening Bulletin, *Harrisburg correspondent,
midnight, June 16, 1863*

Although less in prominence compared to major Northern cities such as
Philadelphia, Baltimore and Washington, D.C., Harrisburg was a target
of Southern invasion more than once.[226] Twice during the war, Harrisburg was
seriously threatened by Confederate forces, and in the last days of June 1863,
Confederate cavalry neared within several miles of the city. In retrospect, it
is not surprising that General Robert E. Lee advised subordinate Richard S.
Ewell in June 1863, "If Harrisburg comes within your means, capture it."[227]
The city was a thriving road and railroad hub—both means of transportation
emanated from Harrisburg to numerous major Northern cities. Not only could
political capital be gained by knocking off a Northern capital, but disrupting
Camp Curtin also meant disrupting the flow of Yankee reinforcements to the
front lines.

The first swipe at Harrisburg came in the fall of 1862. Lee's triumphant
Army of Northern Virginia crossed the Potomac in early September and for
some time roamed the Old Line State unopposed. This created considerable
panic throughout the North, particularly in Harrisburg, which many
understandably feared was a potential target of Lee's invasion. Pennsylvania

governor Andrew G. Curtin warned his constituents of the serious threat posed to the Keystone State in a proclamation on September 4. As the Southern progress came nearer the state border, Curtin issued a second proclamation on September 11, calling for fifty thousand men to defend the state. The following day, Mayor William H. Kepner issued a proclamation of his own, restricting all "able bodied" men from leaving the city unless as a soldier. Harrisburg was under martial law.[228]

Among the residents of the state capital to volunteer their services was Harrisburg native Colonel Henry McCormick. The eldest child of prominent Harrisburg resident, attorney and business tycoon James McCormick Sr., Henry was born in Harrisburg on March 10, 1831. He attended both Harrisburg Academy and Captain Alden Partridge's Military Institute before graduating from Yale in 1852. After his graduation, young Henry began studying law with his father, but he soon determined that "future success could be better attained in the pursuit of commercial and manufacturing interests," prompting him to abandon his legal studies. McCormick quickly began dabbling in the iron industry, and after a careful examination of "all the details" of the Reading furnace, Henry purchased interests in furnaces near Marietta. In 1857, the Keystone or Paxton Furnace south of Harrisburg came under Henry's "management and control."

At the outset of the war, he raised and captained the Lochiel Greys— Company F, 25th Pennsylvania. After the Greys' three-month stint was up, Henry returned home to Harrisburg, where he found himself as invasion threatened his native city. Since Governor Curtin issued his first proclamation on September 4, "home guard" companies from various wards of the city had been drilling each afternoon. "Rumors of coming danger filled the air," later reminisced one Harrisburger, "and for a week or ten days companies had been organized in most of the wards of the city, and every afternoon was spent drilling." Word of Curtin's September 11 call reached these Harrisburg companies at the conclusion of their afternoon drill that same day, and on the morning of September 13, the 1st Pennsylvania Militia Regiment was organized on the capitol grounds, with thirty-one-year-old Henry McCormick at its head. Later that same evening, Colonel McCormick led his regiment—composed of three Harrisburg companies and similar outfits from Shiremanstown, Mechanicsburg, Carlisle and other various localities— down the Cumberland Valley Railroad to Chambersburg. Among the ranks of McCormick's regiment was the unflappable George Bergner, who put his money where his mouth was. Bergner, Harrisburg's postmaster and the proprietor of the *Telegraph*, joined the outfit as a private in Company K.[229]

Militiamen from across the state began to arrive in Harrisburg by the masses shortly after Curtin's September 11 proclamation. "From Saturday evening [September 13] in the night which followed, and all day on Sunday, as fast as one train of cars on the Pennsylvania railroad, the Lebanon Valley [Philadelphia and Reading] and the Northern Central could discharge its living cargo, another steamed into the city ready to contribute the same freight of living, enthusiastic and brave men," detailed the *Telegraph*. The capitol grounds soon became a makeshift camp. Tents were pitched all across the picturesque land, and the medical department even erected a hospital tent "immediately in front" of the state arsenal, located just south of the capitol itself. The scene was somewhat reminiscent of the war's early days in April 1861, before the establishment of Camp Curtin. This was different, though; Camp Curtin, now more than one year old, was filled to its limits, and the overflow of militia troops crowded the city.[230]

Also reminiscent of those early days was the noise and commotion created by the hundreds and thousands of militiamen cramming into Harrisburg proper. "We did not sleep much," recalled Henry F. Charles, a militiaman quartered on the second floor of the capitol, "as the boys were singing and dancing just as if they were at some great frolic."[231] "Everything looks warlike here," penned Captain Samuel Riddle of the Duquesne Light Infantry, one of the many companies encamped on the capitol grounds. "Troops are arriving in every train."[232] With the dense crowds thronging the capitol, some defenders took matters into their own hands. One company marched from the capitol grounds to a field near the city where the corn had already been cut and shucked. Without permission, the militiamen "tore down fences, made temporary tents of the rails, and thatched them with corn stalks" and christened the site Camp Cornstalk.[233]

Although it seemed in the eyes of Harrisburg's citizenry that this surfeit of defenders had surely reached its crest by the morning of September 15, it had not. "We attempted yesterday morning [September 15] to give our readers an idea of the condition of the camps and public grounds in the city," reported the editors of the *Telegraph*.

But all we wrote last evening would fail in coming anything like near a proper estimate of the actual condition of affairs yesterday and last night. From early dawn until the small hours of the night, the trains on the different railroad[s] had been arriving with their patriotic freight, until we now have troops from every county in the State. Camp Curtin is full to overflowing—the capitol grounds are now literally covered with tents—the Senate and House of Representatives are used as barracks—every room in the Capital [sic] *not occupied for other purposes, is now filled with troops—the vacant rooms in the Court House are appropriated to the soldiers.*

The paper likened the city's assortment of hotels to beehives "swarming" with officers and enlisted men. It also observed that "the State Capital is one vast camp."[234]

The officer marked with the arduous task of organizing this jumbled mass of men was Brigadier General John Fulton Reynolds. The Lancaster native and West Point graduate had been dragged from his post as commander of the celebrated Pennsylvania Reserves division with the Army of the Potomac and placed in command of the militia assembling in Harrisburg. Reynolds was given the nearly impossible assignment of organizing this incoherent body of largely untrained and inexperienced troops in a matter of days and leading them down the Cumberland Valley to protect the Pennsylvanian border from invasion. The West Pointer arrived in Harrisburg on Saturday evening, September 13, and soon got to work organizing the militia gathered in the state capital into regiments. A few days later, Reynolds departed Harrisburg with several regiments of militia, with which he operated throughout southern Pennsylvania and northern Maryland during his roughly two-week span in charge of the state militia. Already irritated after he was forced to temporarily leave his command in the Army of the Potomac, that Reynolds was discontent with the militia he commanded is clear in his private correspondence. Just two days after he was relieved of his duties with the state militia, he wrote, "My own private opinion is, however, that if the militia of Pennsylvania is to be depended upon to defend the state from invasion, they had better all stay at home, they can be of no use in any military point of view if they are to act as they did here, every man to decide for himself whether he will obey the orders given."[235]

Several decades later, early twentieth-century Harrisburg columnist A. Boyd Hamilton—whose family went back four generations in Harrisburg and possessed considerable knowledge of the city's Civil War history—opined that the scare and excitement experienced in September 1862 benefited the city during the following summer, when a more serious invasion threatened Harrisburg. "A year later," he wrote, "the city was again thrown into a turmoil by the second invasion, but was better prepared for it."[236] An interesting statement by a knowledgeable fellow, but was Harrisburg truly more prepared for invasion come June 1863?

Colonel Henry McCormick. *U.S. Army Military History Institute.*

One thing is certain. The news of Lee's second invasion of the North did indeed throw Harrisburg into turmoil. Governor Curtin had issued his first of three proclamations that month, confirming rumors of a Southern invasion, on June 12. Three days later, he issued his second proclamation, with a notably more serious tone, calling for fifty thousand men to defend the state. Before Curtin's second proclamation, considerable hints were given the citizenry of Harrisburg as to the potential seriousness of the upcoming invasion. On June 11, Major General Darius Nash Couch, a West Pointer and most recently a corps commander in the Army of the Potomac, left Washington en route for Harrisburg. Upon his arrival in the city, Couch assumed command of the newly formed Department of the Susquehanna, designed to defend all land east of Johnstown and the Laurel Mountains. It did not take long for the West Point graduate to recognize the bleakness of the situation—the prospect of defending Harrisburg at that moment was woeful at best, and this prompted Curtin's second proclamation on June 15. Response to the governor's call for volunteers from within the state was lacking, but discussions between the War Department and New York and New Jersey did result in the promise of troops to come to the aid of the state capital. While he waited for the militia to arrive, Couch set to work constructing fortifications on Bridgeport Heights, on the opposite side of the river and overlooking Harrisburg.[237]

Initially, a combination of remarkable calmness and apathy was the general mood about the city, even as Couch arrived and Curtin issued his first proclamation. In describing the general "feeling" about Harrisburg on June 14, the editors of the *Patriot* wrote:

> *The feeling which prevailed in town…was more calm and business like than it has been heretofore under like circumstances. There was stir and bustle enough, but no unbecoming panic or confusion. The leading men were busily at work in preparing for the worst emergency…Of course, all sorts of absurd rumors were flying, gaining strength as they went, and that spirit of extravagant exaggeration, so inseparable from such a state of affairs as that in which we now find ourselves, obtained a strong lodgment in the minds of the masses. But, in the main, the conduct of the people was calm and determined…There is no strength, but positive weakness, in frenzy and flurry.*[238]

At 11:00 a.m. on June 15, the courthouse bell announced that a gathering of the citizens was "desired to make proper preparation to meet any rebel force that might invade our borders, and this city in particular." The conference enticed several notables to appear, including Governor Curtin, General Couch and the late secretary of war and part-time Harrisburg resident Simon Cameron. The latter first appeared and suggested that Curtin and Couch be requested to make an appearance. Curtin took the floor first and, after

Major General Darius N. Couch.
U.S. Army Military History Institute.

an introduction from the *Telegraph* proprietor and fellow Republican George Bergner, "explained the state of affairs, and urged all to prepare at once for self defence." After Curtin, Couch made an appearance, encouraging every man to lend a hand in the construction of the fortifications across the city. A committee was formed with the goal of rallying citizens for the defense of the city and met in the courthouse at 4:00 p.m., several hours after the first meeting had adjourned. Mayor A.L. Roumfort spoke briefly, directing all who were willing to assist in constructing fortifications across the river to line up in front of the courthouse. "This appeal was largely responded to," recorded the *Patriot*, "and a strong force, bearing picks and spades, soon after crossed the [Camelback] bridge to the [Bridgeport] heights opposite."[239]

This group of patriotic citizens crested Bridgeport Heights opposite the city, where civilian engineers directed the work. The correspondent for the *Philadelphia Daily Evening Bulletin* stationed in Harrisburg estimated the number of civilian volunteers at "about" one thousand. Noted pianist Louis Moreau

Gottschalk, who was visiting the city while on tour, placed the number at three thousand, more likely than not an exaggeration. Throughout the night, those who remained in Harrisburg could clearly discern the "fires of the working parties engaged in throwing up entrenchments" on the opposite bank that illuminated Bridgeport Heights. However, the patriotic citizenry soon discovered that the hill was made up of shale, which rendered their assignment of moving earth extremely difficult. Further, stumbling around in the darkness on such a steep hill was clearly dangerous, but it proved deadly for one individual. Louis Drexler, an employee in Eppley's dry goods store in Market Square, was one of the citizens who volunteered to work on the entrenchments. After working late into the night, he started for home. Instead of descending the hill via the traditional and lengthy route through a field that led to the Carlisle Pike, Drexel used a path that had been created by the First City Zouaves under Captain Asbury Awl when the Harrisburg company was stationed on the heights the previous fall. In the darkness, Drexel lost his footing and tumbled down the cut of the Northern Central Railway, "breaking his back and almost every bone in his body," and he died shortly thereafter. During the course of the night, most of the civilian volunteers returned to Harrisburg, their places later filled by employees of the Pennsylvania Railroad and Canal and African American laborers. By dawn the following morning, a reporter for the *New York Tribune* found only three hundred men at work on the entrenchments.[240]

From the standpoint of Harrisburg's citizenry, the events of June 15 erased any doubts they had entertained about the seriousness of the coming campaign. Particularly intriguing is the response of the city's population. Widespread pandemonium enveloped Harrisburg on Tuesday, June 16. A number of factors led to the panic—among them were the spreading news of Curtin's June 15 proclamation and the construction of the fortifications opposite the city, supplemented by the mad dash across the Susquehanna that many Cumberland Valley farmers were making in an attempt to evade the Southern army. En route to Harrisburg in the early afternoon hours of June 16, pianist Gottschalk found the means of transportation one mile west of the Susquehanna "completely obstructed by freight trains, wagons of all sorts." The celebrated musician arrived at the Jones House, which he found "overrun by a noisy crowd, in which I recognize many New York reporters, sent in haste by the great journals in the hopes of furnishing their readers with sensational news." From his hotel room window, Gottschalk could grasp the seriousness of the situation: "I see all along the river great clouds of dust; it is from the herds of cattle which the frightened farmers are driving towards the mountains, in hopes of hiding them from the rebels."[241]

"During this morning [June 16] a perfect panic prevailed, extending to all classes of people, and resulting in the grandest demand for railroad tickets ever witnessed in this city," detailed the *Philadelphia Daily Evening Bulletin* correspondent in Harrisburg. Absurd rumors spread through town, placing the Confederates "just over the river" at Carlisle. In reality, only Southern cavalry under Brigadier General Albert G. Jenkins had yet crossed into Pennsylvania, and Jenkins had only reached as far as Chambersburg. "Trunks were piled up at the depots six feet in height, for nearly a square, and hundreds if not thousands of people eagerly awaited the hour of the departure of the various trains." Wagon trains from Major General Robert H. Milroy's division—which had been greatly embarrassed in the course of its defeat at the Second Battle of Winchester several days earlier—passed through the city, where they finally found some small semblance of safety in the chaos that had enveloped Harrisburg. "During the entire afternoon Market street was occupied with army wagons from Milroy's division," the *Daily Evening Bulletin* correspondent recorded, "which rumbled across the old [Camelback] bridge and from thence past the railroad depot and out to a camp on the other [east] side of the of the canal." The passage of the wagon train stirred up considerable amounts of dust. "For several hours this wagon train completely filled Market street, giving the spectators a far better idea of the dust, turmoil and fatigue of war than they could get in any other way." In the meantime, the state archives, portraits "and other valuables" were removed to Philadelphia for safekeeping. Similarly, the "extensive and valuable collection of books" in the state library was also sent to Philadelphia. Some vague form of regularity was still present, however, in those who opted not to flee. As the *Daily Evening Bulletin* correspondent closed his report on the evening of June 16, he added, "Democratic politicians are drinking at the hotel bars, and the regular routine of night life at the Capital is in full progress."[242]

After the panic that ensued on June 16, the mood in Harrisburg apparently calmed to a degree. One traveling New York businessman determined to visit the Keystone State capital on the evening of June 16 after learning of the commotion that had occurred there. "[A]fter we reached Harrisburg we found that the excitement was much less than on the evening previous [June 16]," he recorded, the reason for the calm being reports that the city's Southern antagonists had retreated.[243] However, by nightfall on June 17, scores of Pennsylvania militia companies had arrived in Harrisburg, creating a scene familiar to that during the Maryland Campaign the previous fall—militia companies camped about the city and on the capitol grounds. Additionally, Democrats were running rampant with excitement, having nominated Judge George Woodward to oppose Governor Curtin in the upcoming election that same evening. "If possible, there is more noise and confusion in Harrisburg to-night than there was at this time last night," noted the *Daily Evening Bulletin* correspondent in his daily report.

> *Excited and inebriate Democrats are parading Market and other streets and singing, while crowds of soldiers are passing along or peacefully sleeping on the pavements. The capitol grounds are crowded with sleepers of both characters, the volunteers not having yet been assigned camping grounds, though arrangement will be made during the night for the accommodation... Troops are crowding into town from all quarters and every train brings accessions to their number. Market street, even at this late hour, resounds to the tramp of resolute men who have gathered to resist the onward progress of the rebel hordes. At every step one takes he is apt to tread upon a brother Pennsylvanian, and every hotel bar room into which one peers seems to be filled with warlike strangers.* [244]

Twenty-four hours later—at midnight on June 18—the same correspondent with the *Daily Evening Bulletin* penned yet another detailed description. Still, few of the residents who had fled in the panic of June 16 had returned, "but there are enough of the female portion of the inhabitants left to remind one that this is still Harrisburg." The streets remained thronged with knapsack-bearing crowds, "and every train which comes in adds to the general mass." The "shelves of the shops and the empty parlors of prominent citizens" appeared "rather doleful," he detailed, "and the closed shutters of many mansions do not enliven the prospect, but we 'still live' and still hope to keep the old flag waving from the dome of the Capitol."[245]

Even despite the construction of earthworks across the city and the panic of June 16, some Harrisburgers remained unconvinced that an invasion truly threatened their city. Citizen Jacob R. Spangler penned a letter on June 18, expressing his doubts about the reports filtering into the city. "[W]e have had another scare here the town has been in excitement the most of this week from reports of Rebbel raids &c. but we have not had the pleasure of Seeing any of the Rebbs yet." Spangler, an unbending Democrat, believed that "all this fuss is got up" by a politically motivated Curtin.[246] Spangler was not alone in his far-reaching opinion—just across the river, a farmer north of New Cumberland annoyed some New York National Guard troops with his radical views. "His politics were of a pronounced 'Copperhead' stripe and had allowed them to affect his common sense so much as to lead him to frequently declare 'that he did not believe there were any rebels in the State and that the whole affair was an election dodge of Andy Curtin,'" recalled one New Yorker. His comments gave the New York troops stationed on his property "quite a satisfaction" to dig a large rifle pit right across his nicely groomed garden.[247]

No love was lost between Governor Curtin and Simon Cameron, bitter political rivals from years past. The two, along with General Couch, were forced to work together in order to defend the city. Although Cameron had stated in another public meeting at the courthouse that he was "ready to shoulder a musket and go as a private under the Governor," in more secluded situations, their true bitter feelings were exposed. "There is no good feeling between any two of them," detailed Major General William B. Franklin, a York native who visited Harrisburg in late June on a purely speculative basis. "Cameron abuses Curtin, and Curtin is not quite so open in abuse but is just as bitter as Cameron. Couch does not feel comfortable under the circumstances of course, but I think tries to do his best."[248]

Militia and National Guard troops began to crowd Harrisburg soon after construction on the fortifications opposite the city had begun. Upon their arrival, many of Harrisburg's defenders expressed their displeasure at the apparent lethargy and indifference of the city's residents. "The residents of the capital itself appeared listless," opined John Lockwood of the 23rd New York State National Guard. "Hundreds of strong men in the prime of life loitered in the public thoroughfares, and gaped at our passing columns as indifferently as if we had come as conquerors…Panic-stricken by the reported approach on the enemy, the poltroons of the city had closed their houses and stores, offered their stocks of merchandize for sale at ruinous prices, and were thinking of nothing in their abject fear except how to escape with their worthless lives and their property."[249]

Another New York guardsman penned that "little desire" was entertained by most New Yorkers to visit Harrisburg. Not only had they been received unceremoniously, but they also accused the city's merchants of jacking up their prices especially for them, charging for glasses of water.[250] In reality, this unpatriotic practice had been going on before the summer of 1863, but it apparently increased around the time of the invasion and arrival of additional troops. The New Yorkers were not alone in their criticism. Future governor Samuel Pennypacker, who had journeyed to the state capital in the

Simon Cameron. *Author's collection.*

ranks of a militia company from Phoenixville, could not repress a "feeling of displeasure…when thinking that we had come a hundred miles from a sense of duty while those in the immediate vicinity of the Capital, who had every incentive to arouse themselves, were doing nothing."[251]

The critiquing that Harrisburg received at the hands of its defenders was certainly warranted, but the statement that Harrisburgers did nothing for their own defense is not entirely true. Several companies did come from the capital city during the summer of 1863; two outfits in particular raised from the city saw various forms of action during the ensuing campaign. A company of cavalry that was christened the "Curtin Guards" was formed at the livery office of Frank A. Murray on Fourth Street near Walnut. A detachment from Murray's outfit was ambushed—with several men captured and wounded—in a skirmish southwest of Carlisle at Stone Tavern. The company was also present immediately preceding surrender of Mechanicsburg on June 28.[252] The other company, the "First City Zouaves," was reactivated after having been mustered out the previous month with the 127th Pennsylvania. Led by Captain F. Asbury Awl, during its service in the 127th as Company A, the outfit never served with the other nine companies of the regiment in the field. Awl's company had founded Camp Simmons, north of Camp Curtin, and Camp Dodge, on Bridgeport Heights opposite Harrisburg. In the predawn hours of July 2, 1863, the company—stationed in Harrisburg along the riverbank in front of the Harris-Cameron Mansion—forced the surrender of a man rowing the Susquehanna, accused of being a Southern spy.[253]

The "high tide" of the Confederate thrust toward Harrisburg occurred on June 29 when Virginia cavalrymen belonging to the brigade of General Albert G. Jenkins pushed back Yankee skirmishers at Oyster's Point, less than three miles from Harrisburg. The following day, Jenkins's men met defeat at the Battle of Sporting Hill—a minor engagement just more than five miles west of the capital city—before retiring toward Gettysburg, which the Virginia cavaliers reached in the early evening hours of July 1. Only fifteen miles away had been two divisions of Lieutenant General Richard S. Ewell's Second Corps, amounting to roughly fifteen thousand men, who on June 29 were preparing to march for Harrisburg, only to be retarded by orders from General Lee, directing the corps to head for a small town in Adams County.

In Harrisburg, rude preparations had been taken to defend the city if Ewell had, as expected, assaulted the state capital. The earthworks on Bridgeport Heights were rendered acceptable by a few days' hacking and were proudly christened Fort Washington, which was supplemented by another series of earthworks, called Fort Couch or Fort Henry Clay. Spans of the Camelback and Cumberland Valley Railroad bridges had been cut, ready to drop on a moment's notice to prevent Southern invaders from crossing the Susquehanna with ease. The city was once again under martial law. It was only when the Confederates were at the very outskirts of the city that troop movements on the opposite side of the river were made "strictly confidential." Passes were not issued to citizens and especially reporters, who were "positively forbidden to cross or in any way to make use of information concerning the operations of the Army of the Susquehanna." As the *Telegraph* chastised, "[E]very man who is really anxious to know all about the movements of the Army of the Susquehanna, can gratify himself by enlisting in one of the companies now forming." The Gettysburg Campaign, however, was all but over for the citizenry of Harrisburg when Ewell and Jenkins departed the city's front. "During the battle," recalled Harrisburger Francis Hoy, "Front street was packed with humanity, as the cannonading was very distinctly heard here." And for weeks and months following the battle, Harrisburg cared for the wounded soldiers. "I remember very distinctly," Hoy continued, "the following Sabbath that the only services held in our churches was the singing of the doxology, pronouncing the benediction, and the handing out of lint to be picked and material to make bandages for the wounded."[254]

Chapter 7

Harrisburg After the Civil War

Harrisburg is rapidly becoming what it was before the opening of the rebellion—a quiet, orderly city—but with a great improvement in its business affairs, and an enlarged population…During a period of four years and a half our citizens have been accustomed to see the "blue coats" in their midst. Frequently our streets have been thronged with the military, who rushed by thousands in times of danger, in answer to the repeated calls of their country for help: and again thousands of returning heroes have caused our city to present the appearance of a great military centre. The excitement incident to the approach of a powerful enemy, and the threatened destruction of life and property by an invading foe, will never be forgotten. All these scenes are past, and we are again favored with peace. Our streets have resumed their wonted quiet; the cry "to arms," is no longer heard, the fears of an invasion and the destruction of happy home, are felt no more, and armed soldiers have almost disappeared from our midst. The contrast is such as only can be realized by those who witnessed the varied scenes through which our people have passed, and which we trust may never occur again.[255]

So wrote the editors of the *Telegraph* in the waning days of 1865. As the year 1865 came to a close, so did Harrisburg's involvement in the American Civil War. By November, only the 6th Regiment United States Veteran Volunteers—known as "Hancock's 6th"—remained in Camp Curtin. Two weeks into November, the 6th departed for Washington. "Camp Curtin is now deserted," reported the *Telegraph*, "and will no longer be used as a rendezvous for troops. The Government property belonging to the camp will be disposed of, and the grounds appropriated to other uses." While the 6th was not the last regiment to pass through Harrisburg, it was an awkward feeling for the citizenry of Harrisburg to think that Camp Curtin was entirely deserted.[256]

Indeed, in the past four years, much had gone on in the city of Harrisburg. In Camp Curtin particularly, thousands upon thousands of soldiers had been quartered there during their first initiation into soldiery or as they completed their stint in the army, waiting to be mustered out. Naturally, the question arises of exactly how many troops passed through Camp Curtin during the course of the war. In 1922, the camp's earliest historian, Reverend Alvin S. Williams of Harrisburg, deemed it a "conservative estimate" that 300,000 soldiers passed through the camp.[257] Williams's statement has been generally accepted by historians ever since. Reverend Williams could claim the title of being Camp Curtin's first historian. His twenty-three-page history was compiled in anticipation of the dedication of a statue to Governor Curtin on the site of the camp. Williams's research on the camp did not delve into accounts from the ranks; instead, his narrative was based almost entirely on state and national government records, but nonetheless was well done save a few minor errors. Leading up to the dedication, a Harrisburg newspaper reported that Williams's history "contains not only many valuable matters, but first-hand information representing much labor." Reverend Williams himself even admitted that his pamphlet was imperfect in some respects, owing to "the incompleteness of State and National records." He also expressed "the hope that before it is too late a more comprehensive study of the cam may be accomplished."[258]

By 1922, when the Curtin memorial was dedicated, the grounds of Camp Curtin had been developed as the city of Harrisburg sprouted northward. Early on, the camp remained a vacant lot, occasionally rented by various groups needing open ground. In 1870, the Harrisburg Cricket Club rented "some vacant ground" on the old campsite.[259] During this period, a number of abandoned buildings from the camp remained standing; the camp hospital reportedly stood into the early 1880s.[260] For years, the desire existed among Harrisburg citizens and veterans to set aside the campground, but no action was taken. For some time, a memorial arch was "seriously considered" for placement at the intersection of Sixth and Maclay Streets, near the historic entrance of Camp Curtin, but like most efforts to preserve the camp, nothing came of it. Eventually, as the beginning of the twentieth century neared, the city enlarged through Camp Curtin, and any hope to preserve the grounds

This 1889 photograph shows the demolition of the market sheds, with the Bolton (Buehler) House in the background. *Historical Society of Dauphin County.*

was lost. The memory of the camp, however, was not, and a number of the buildings later erected on the site bore the camp's name. The Camp Curtin School was located at the southeast corner of Sixth and Woodbine Streets. Opposite the school, the Camp Curtin Memorial Church was named in honor of the encampment.[261]

As did Camp Curtin, the rest of Harrisburg changed rapidly as well. By 1900, the Camelback Bridge had already endured significant damage. In 1846, its eastern section was destroyed by flood, and it was repaired and reopened in September 1847. Shortly after the war, in May 1866, the eastern section was enveloped by flames, but once again it was rebuilt and reopened, in November 1867. However, the old Camelback was dealt its final blow when both sections were destroyed by a flood on March 2, 1902. The Market Street Bridge, still in operation today, later took its place.

Other relics of the 1860s Harrisburg also disappeared. The Pennsylvania Railroad demolished its wartime station, which had transported thousands of soldiers to and from Harrisburg, erecting a new structure in 1887 a short distance farther west of the wartime building that is still in use today.

Similarly, the wartime Philadelphia and Reading depot was replaced by a new station in 1904 that was in use for roughly fifty years before it was razed. In 1889, the market sheds were removed from Harrisburg's Market Square. In 1897, the capitol was destroyed by fire but was rebuilt and rededicated in 1906. Grand Army of the Republic Posts 58 (J.F. Hartranft), 116 (S.G. Simmons) and 520 (D.R. Stephens) were all present throughout the city, but they eventually vanished as the Civil War veterans disappeared with the passing years. Henceforth, the story of Harrisburg and the Civil War lives on through the letters, diaries and the recollections of the men and women who experienced it firsthand.[262]

Notes

ABBREVIATIONS

CWD	Civil War Document Collection, USAMHI
DPU	*Harrisburg Daily Patriot and Union*
DT	*Harrisburg Daily Telegraph*
ET	*Harrisburg Evening Telegraph*
GNMP	Gettysburg National Military Park
HCWRT	Harrisburg Civil War Round Table Collection, USAMHI
HSDC	Historical Society of Dauphin County
HT	*Harrisburg Telegraph*
USAMHI	U.S. Army Military History Institute

Harrisburg's Initial Responses to the Civil War

1. *DPU*, "Local News," April 15, 1861.
2. Washington, *President Washington's Diaries*, 56.
3. Glazier, *Peculiarities of American Cities*, 199–200; Book, *Northern Rendezvous*, 1–3.
4. Morgan, *Annals of Harrisburg*, 263–64; Eggert, *Harrisburg Industrializes*, 62–63.
5. Inglewood, *Then and Now in Harrisburg*, 83–85; Morgan, *Annals of Harrisburg*, 264.
6. Eggert, *Harrisburg Industrializes*, 26–30, 40–41.
7. Dickens, *American Notes*, 2: 35–36.
8. Inglewood, *Then and Now in Harrisburg*, 151–55.
9. Steinmetz and Hoffsommer, *This Was Harrisburg*, 48; Book, *Northern Rendezvous*, 80.
10. *DPU*, "Our Hotels," December 15, 1860.
11. Ibid.; Morgan, *Annals of Harrisburg*, 451.
12. Morgan, *Annals of Harrisburg*, 452; Dickens, *American Notes*, 2:36; Inglewood, *Then and Now in Harrisburg*, 60–61; *DPU*, "Hotels," October 16, 1860; *DPU*, "A Fine Restaurant," December 8, 1860; *DPU*, "Our Hotels," December 15, 1860; *HT*, "Harrisburg in the Days of Civil War," October 3, 1905.
13. Morgan, *Annals of Harrisburg*, 429.
14. Ibid., 428, 451; Inglewood, *Then and Now in Harrisburg*, 57–58; *DPU*, "Our Hotels," December 15, 1860; Cornwallis, *Royalty in the New World*, 181–82.
15. McClure, *Abraham Lincoln and Men of War Times*, 43–50.
16. Book, *Northern Rendezvous*, 5, 14–15; Morgan, *Annals of Harrisburg*, 249–50, 254–55, 257–58.
17. Book, *Northern Rendezvous*, 1; Glazier, *Peculiarities of American Cities*, 200.
18. Eggert, *Harrisburg Industrializes*, 49–69, 85–86.
19. Steinmetz and Hoffsommer, *This Was Harrisburg*, 59; Molyneux, *Quill of the Wild Goose*, 293.
20. Eggert, *Harrisburg Industrializes*, 300–301; Egle et al., *Commemorative Biographical Encyclopedia*, 338.
21. *DT*, "The Patriot and Union," April 13, 1861.
22. *DT*, "The Commencement of Hostilities," April 13, 1861.
23. *DPU*, "Local News," April 15, 1861.

24. Ibid.
25. *DT*, "From Washington!," April 15, 1861.
26. *DT*, "The Union Feeling in Harrisburg," April 16, 1861; *DPU*, "Meeting to Sustain the National Government," April 17, 1861; Morgan, *Annals of Harrisburg*, 262.
27. Isaac R. Dunkelberger, "Reminiscences and Personal Experiences of the Great Rebellion," GNMP.
28. Ibid.; Dunkelberger recorded that he arrived in Harrisburg on April 16; however, as evidenced by his accounts of the days immediately following his arrival, he was often off on his dates. Compared to various newspaper accounts, April 18 is the only date that fits his account. This also takes into consideration that he reported his arrival at Camp Curtin that evening (April 16) when the camp was not founded until April 18.
29. Ibid.; Egle, *Notes and Queries*, Annual Volume, 1896, 144–45. One month into his service with the Cameron Guards, Eyster received an appointment as a captain in the 18th U.S. Infantry. However, he chose to serve out his three-month term with the Cameron Guards before accepting this post. At the Battle of Missionary Ridge, he was shot through the ankle; at Chickamauga, a bullet "tore away part of his nose"; and at Chattanooga, "in a desperate cavalry battle he received a sabre cut on the right hand and a bayonet wound on the left hand." Despite his wounds, Eyster survived the war and died in Harrisburg in 1896.
30. *DPU*, "William B. Sipes, Esq.," April 22, 1861; *DT*, "Harrisburg and the War," May 24, 1861.
31. *DT*, "Departure of Troops," May 9, 1861; *DT*, "From the Federal Capital," May 23, 1861; *DT*, "Military Affairs," May 4, 1861; *DPU*, "The Verbeke Rifles," April 25, 1861.
32. *DT*, "Departure of the Cameron and State Capital Guards," April 22, 1861.
33. *DT*, "The Stars and Stripes," April 17, 1861; *DT*, "The Patriotism of Harrisburg," April 20, 1861; *DT*, "Over the Prison," May 1, 1861; *DT*, "Shirts for the Soldiers," May 24, 1861; *DPU*, "Haversacks," April 22, 1861; *DPU*, "List," April 24, 1861.
34. Calvin Pardee to Dear Pa, April 18, 1861, Pardee-Robinson Collection, USAMHI.
35. "Our Army Correspondence," *The Globe*, April 23, 1861.
36. Thompson, *First Defenders*, 12, 113; Charles C. Pollock to Dear Ma, April 19, 1861, CWD, USAMHI.

37. Miscellaneous newspaper clippings, German Scrapbook, HSDC; Inglewood, *Then and Now in Harrisburg*, 94; Williams, *Ceremonies at the Dedication*, 7–8.

38. Egle et al., *Commemorative Biographical Encyclopedia*, 244–45; Rowell, *Yankee Cavalrymen*, 19.

39. Trussell, "Brig. Gen. Joseph F. Knipe," 4–5.

40. Ibid., 1–4.

41. Inglewood, *Then and Now in Harrisburg*, 89—90. Around the turn of the twentieth century, Ridge Road became Sixth Street.

42. *DT*, "The County Fair," September 11, 1860.

43. Miscellaneous newspaper clippings, German Scrapbook, HSDC. This account left by Knipe's daughter, Teresa (later Teresa Hogentogler), is from an interview conducted in October 1922 as she prepared to attend the dedication of the Camp Curtin Memorial. Teresa identifies her sister, who was also present, as Ida (later Ida Gastrock). According to Bates's *History of Pennsylvania Volunteers*, Company G, 3rd Pennsylvania Infantry (from Johnstown) was the first company to enter Camp Curtin. See Bates, *History of Pennsylvania Volunteers*, 1:32.

44. Williams, *Ceremonies at the Dedication*, 14; *DPU*, "Military News," April 20, 1861.

45. *Central Press*, "The Late News," May 9, 1861.

46. *Central Press*, "From Camp Curtin," May 9, 1861; Dunkelberger, "Reminiscences and Personal Experiences," GNMP; *DPU*, "A Thrilling Incident at Camp Curtin!," April 22, 1861. Documenting this encounter has proved extremely difficult. Accounts conflict on a date. The incident had to have occurred before April 25. The latter is evident by a note above Muffley's letter in the Bellefonte *Central Press* that explains that the "following communication from a Bellefonte volunteer then in Camp Curtin, was intended for the Press of the 25th ult., but did not reach us in time, and having been in type for last Thursday's issue, which did not appear, we nevertheless give it [to] our readers to-day." This dates Muffley's letter to before April 25. The only Saturday before April 25 yet after April 18 (when the camp was founded) is April 20, which the *Patriot and Union* also notes as the date. Dunkelberger reported that his company arrived in Camp Curtin on April 16—obviously incorrect, considering that the camp was not established until April 18. He then placed the date of the incident at Camp Curtin as 10:00 a.m. on April 17, which also is one day before Camp Curtin was founded; hence, Dunkelberger is obviously off on his dates. However, when he did enter Camp Curtin, he

remained there for several days until departing on the evening of April 20, and he certainly could have seen the eagle fly over the camp earlier that same afternoon.

47. Montgomery, *Historical and Biographical Annals*, 1:327–28; Heitman, *Historical Register*, 1:587; Warner, *Generals in Blue*, 259–60; *DT*, "Description of Camp Curtin," April 22, 1861.

48. Montgomery, *Historical and Biographical Annals*, 1:328; Warner, *Generals in Blue*, 259–60.

49. *DT*, Miscellaneous Section, April 30, 1861. Although Williams initially assumed command of the camp, it remains unclear that he ever took on the title of camp commandant.

50. *HT*, "Harrisburg in the Days of Civil War," October 3, 1905; Kelker, *History of Dauphin County*, 1:539.

51. *DT*, "We Understand," April 24, 1861.

52. *ET*, "Annual Report of the Ladies' Union Relief Association of Harrisburg, Pa.," September 17, 1863; *Democratic Banner*, "Letter from a Soldier," October 12, 1863; Kelker, *History of Dauphin County*, 1:532–33; Egle et al., *Commemorative Biographical Encyclopedia*, 38–39.

53. *ET*, "The Sick Soldiers' Rest," August 24, 1864.

54. Edgar A. Walters, "Off to the War: A Year in the Ranks," HCWRT, USAMHI.

55. McCalmont, *Extracts from Letters*, 93.

56. Bently Kutz Diary, July 15, 1864, HCWRT, USAMHI.

57. Gansevoort, *Memorial of Henry Sanford Gansevoort*, 97.

58. Chamberlin, *Cleaning Up the Muss*, 11–13.

59. Lyman Beebe to Dear Respected Wife and Children, November 12, 1862, CWD, USAMHI.

60. Kerr, *Civil War Surgeon*, 22–23.

61. Eggert, *Harrisburg Industrializes*, 75–81.

62. Sprenger, *Concise History*, 322; *HT*, "Harrisburg in the Days of Civil War," October 3, 1905; *Philadelphia Press*, "State Items," August 10, 1865.

63. *HT*, "Harrisburg in the Days of Civil War," October 3, 1905.

CAMP CURTIN AND ITS SUBSIDIARIES

64. Dornblaser, *Sabre Strokes*, 22–23.

65. Knipe was aide-de-camp to Williams, and his rank was that of major, which is consistently stated in some of General Keim's published orders. See *DT*, "General Orders—No. 2," February 9, 1861.

66. *HT*, "Harrisburg in the Days of Civil War," October 3, 1905; *Central Press*, "From Camp Curtin," May 9, 1861; Holmes, *Pages*, 57–58; miscellaneous newspaper clippings, German Scrapbook, HSDC.

67. Miscellaneous newspaper clippings, Philip German Map of Camp Curtin, German Scrapbook, HSDC.

68. *DT*, "Description of Camp Curtin," April 22, 1861.

69. Ibid.; *Central Press*, "From Camp Curtin," May 9, 1861; *The Agitator*, "More About Camp Curtin," June 5, 1861; German Map of Camp Curtin, German Scrapbook, HSDC. During the summer of 1863, Colonel James Beaver was detailed as camp commandant by Major General Darius Couch to organize hastily raised militia companies gathered there. Beaver recorded that the "headquarters of the camp were upstairs but I was unable to mount the stairs" due to a recent wound suffered at the Battle of Chancellorsville, and instead he "seized a vacant building near the gate." Beaver's account verifies that the second story of Floral Hall was used as offices for camp officials throughout the war. See Muffly, *Story of Our Regiment*, 92–93.

70. Several sources clearly state that the hospital had been completed by late April 1861. The earliest mention of the building comes from a letter written about one week after Camp Curtin initially opened. See *Central Press*, "From Camp Curtin," May 9, 1861. As of April 27, "There are some five or six men sick in the hospital at Camp Curtin—none seriously, however. The diseases are such as naturally arise from the change of mode of life." See *DPU*, "The Hospital," April 27, 1861.

71. German Map of Camp Curtin, German Scrapbook, HSDC.

72. *The Agitator*, "More About Camp Curtin," June 5, 1861.

73. *ET*, "Annual Report," September 17, 1863. The association's efforts were halted during the winter of 1862, when an outbreak of smallpox rendered the camp unsafe to enter.

74. *DT*, "Camp Curtin," May 13, 1861; *DPU*, "Camp Curtin," April 24, 1861; *The Agitator*, "More About Camp Curtin," June 5, 1861; German Map of Camp Curtin, German Scrapbook, HSDC.

75. *DT*, "Description of Camp Curtin," April 22, 1861; *DPU*, "Camp Curtin," April 24, 1861.

76. Lucas, *I Seat Myself*, 15.

77. *DPU*, "Barracks Condemned," August 8, 1863; *DPU*, "Camp Curtin," August 27, 1863.

78. *DT*, "Description of Camp Curtin," April 22, 1861; *DPU*, "Camp Curtin," April 24, 1861; *Central Press*, "From Camp Curtin," May 9, 1861; German Map of Camp Curtin, German Scrapbook, HSDC.

79. German Map of Camp Curtin, German Scrapbook, HSDC.

80. Ibid.; Joseph D. Baker to Dear Mother, October 28, 1861, GNMP.

81. *ET*, "Camp Curtin Variola Hospital," August 8, 1863; German Map of Camp Curtin, German Scrapbook, HSDC.

82. *HT*, "Harrisburg in the Days of Civil War," October 3, 1905; miscellaneous newspaper clippings, German Scrapbook, HSDC.

83. *Central Press*, "From Camp Curtin," May 9, 1861.

84. John Milton Bancroft Diary, June 26–July 1, 1861, University of Michigan; J.D. Richardson to unspecified, June 28, 1861, University of Michigan; Edward H.C. Taylor to My Dear Sister, June 31, 1861, University of Michigan. Another account of a Camp Cameron near Harrisburg also exists. In a November 1862 letter from Camp Simmons now in the private collection of James E. Schmick, Sergeant Charles D. Levan of the 178th Pennsylvania Drafted Militia wrote that from the dome of the capitol, he could see "all over the city," including "Camp Simmons and part of Camp Cameron." Both known camps with the latter title were presumably not in operation—only the 4th Michigan left accounts of the first Camp Cameron, while the second was clearly broken up during the winter of 1861–62. Most likely, the camp referred to here as Camp Cameron was actually Camp McClellan, as this letter is postmarked November 11, one day after two cavalry regiments left Camp Simmons for Camp McClellan. Levan even mentioned cavalry "moving from camp this morning" and added that "the men that left…this morning I understand went to Camp Cameron."

85. Samuel J. Alexander to Dear and Much Loved Wife, August 7, 1861, and Alexander to Dear Wife, August 13, 1861, CWD, USAMHI; newspaper clipping from 62nd Pennsylvania Infantry, Graham Family Papers, CWD, USAMHI; *DT*, "Colonel Sam Black's Regiment," August 7, 1861; *Altoona Tribune*, "Our Army Correspondence," September 26, 1861; *HT*, "Harrisburg in the Days of Civil War," October 3, 1905; *DT*, "Camp Cameron," August 15, 1861; *DT*, "Circular," September 23, 1861.

According to citizen Francis Hoy, Camp Cameron "ran from opposite Cameron's woods to Hanna's woods." Hanna's Woods was located south of what later became "Swatara street and east of thirteenth," while Cameron's Woods was situated along present-day Nineteenth Street. See *HT*, "Harrisburg in the Days of Civil War," October 3, 1905; miscellaneous newspaper clippings, German Scrapbook, HSDC. Also, in an August 13 letter to his wife, Samuel Alexander described Camp Cameron: "[W]e are encamped on General Camerons farm about 2 miles from Harrisburg[.] [I]t is a very Pritty place our camp is pitched in a field along side of a wood that was formerly used for Picknicks by the young people of Harrisburg[.] [W]e have a excellent spring of water and a crick running close to our camp for us to wash out cloes in and to Bathe." See Alexander to Dear Wife, August 13, 1861, CWD, USAMHI. Accounts generally concur that the camp was located on a "rolling tract of land." See *DT*, "Camp Cameron," August 15, 1861.

86. *Daily Pittsburgh Gazette and Commercial Journal*, "Letter from Camp Cameron," August 14, 1861; *Daily Pittsburgh Gazette and Commercial Journal*, "Camp Cameron," August 17, 1861; Alexander to Dear Wife, August 13, August 19, 1861, CWD, USAMHI.

87. Alexander to Dear Wife, August 19, 1861, CWD, USAMHI.

88. Ibid., August 22, 1861.

89. *DT*, "Circular," September 23, 1861.

90. *DT*, "Camp Cameron," October 14, 1861.

91. Rumsey, *Mansfield Men*, 20.

92. Dornblaser, *Sabre Strokes*, 14–16.

93. Ibid., 18–19. On the topic of rations in Camp Cameron, Corporal Joseph Higgins of the 76th Pennsylvania noted, "[W]e are all getting as fat and lazy as a set of stall fed pigs." See Joseph Higgins to Dear Sidney, October 7, 1861, CWD, USAMHI.

94. Dornblaser, *Sabre Strokes*, 19–22; Dornblaser, *My Life Story*, 44–49; Rumsey, *Mansfield Men*, 20.

95. Dornblaser, *Sabre Strokes*, 22–23.

96. Ibid., 23–24.

97. Benjamin Steiner to Dear Brother, October 18, 1861, CWD, USAMHI; Rumsey, *Mansfield Men*, 20.

98. Steiner to Dear Brother, October 18, 1861, CWD, USAMHI.

99. *Danville Intelligencer*, "Camp Cameron," November 1, 1861; *Danville Intelligencer*, "Camp Cameron," November 22, 1861.

100. Hewett, *Supplement to the Official Records*, 57:2, 116–17; Orbo W. Palmer to Dear Sister, December 7, 1861, CWD, USAMHI.

101. *Altoona Tribune*, "Our Army Correspondence," September 26, 1861; also see John J. Miller to Dear Brother, November 28, 1861, George Miller Papers, USAMHI, for another mention of Camp Cameron by a member of the 76th Pennsylvania.

102. *Pittsburgh Daily Gazette and Adviser*, "Military Movements," December 12, 1861; *DT*, "Public Sale," March 13, 1862.

103. Lossing, *Memoir of Lieut.-Col. John T. Greble*, 89; Bush, *Short History*, 5–7; Cullum, *Biographical Register*, 1:502–3, 526–27. Bush clearly stated that Camp Greble was founded in June 1861, shortly after Greble's death. However, Lossing quoted Williams as informing his wife of the camp's establishment in September. The 5th was certainly in Harrisburg as of June, and most likely the camp had been established by that time as well. Unfortunately, no manuscript collection of Williams's letters (which evidently exist) has been located by the author. Williams's letters from 1862 were later published by one of his sons, G. Mott Williams, under the title "Documents: Letters of General Thomas Williams, 1862," in the January 1909 edition of the *American Historical Review*.

104. Gansevoort, *Memorial of Henry Sanford Gansevoort*, 30, 97–98.

105. Ibid., 98–99, 102.

106. Ibid., 99–100.

107. Ibid., 100–101.

108. Ibid., 98; *DT*, "Circular," September 23, 1861; *DT*, "Camp Cameron," September 27, 1861; Cullum, *Biographical Register*, 1:526–27 and 2:151–53; *DT*, "The Fifth Artillery," December 13, 1861; *Altoona Tribune*, "Our Army Correspondence," September 26, 1861; Bush, *Short History*, 5–7; *Danville Intelligencer*, "Camp Cameron," November 1, 1861; Hewett, *Supplement to the Official Records*, 57:2, 113–17. Brigadier General James S. Negley assumed command of Camp Cameron on September 6, which raises the question of whether Williams was in command before or after Negley. However, it is clear that Williams was in command by mid-September, and the latest account of him in this role dates from September 27. See *DT*, "Gen. Negley," September 7, 1861; *DT*, "Camp Cameron," September 27, 1861.

109. Porter, *76th Regiment*, 5–6. Porter also noted that "all the troops" within Camp Cameron "except the artillery were under the immediate eye of the Camp Commander." This statement suggests that there was a separate, subaltern commander of the artillery at Camp Greble.

110. See Steiner to Dear Brother, October 18, 1861, CWD, USAMHI.

111. *DT*, "The Fifth Artillery," December 14, 1861.

112. *DT*, "Public Sale of Wooden Barracks!," May 7, 1862.

113. Gansevoort, *Memorial of Henry Sanford Gansevoort*, 100.

114. Ibid., 109–12; *DT*, "Public Sale of Wooden Barracks!," May 7, 1862.

115. Regimental Association, *History of the 127th Regiment*, 23–29. Awl's company, raised form Harrisburg in the spring of 1861, was known as the "First City Zouaves." The company was "armed and equipped by the authorities of the Commonwealth of Pennsylvania, and being part of its militia system, regularly performed the duties incident thereto." Mustered into service on July 26, 1862, the outfit later became Company A, 127th Pennsylvania Volunteers. However, Awl's force never joined the 127th in the field and served its nine months on guard duty at various locations between Harrisburg and Washington, D.C.

116. Ellis, *Norwich University*, 2:221; Cullum, *Biographical Register*, 1:454–55; Bates, *Martial Deeds*, 406–9; genealogy document, Simmons Family Collection, MG 275, HSDC; Simmons, "Reminiscence of My Childhood," Simmons Family Collection, MG 275, HSDC. For confirmation of Simmons's date of marriage, which Bates in *Martial Deeds* mistakes as August 1835, see the family genealogy document in the Simmons Family Collection, MG 275, HSDC.

117. Bates, *Martial Deeds*, 408–9; Cullum, *Biographical Register*, 1:454–55; genealogy document, Simmons Family Collection, MG 275, HSDC.

118. Cullum, *Biographical Register*, 1:454–55; miscellaneous newspaper clippings, German Scrapbook, HSDC.

119. Miscellaneous newspaper clippings, German Scrapbook, HSDC.

120. Bates, *Martial Deeds*, 408; Cullum, *Biographical Register*, 1:455; *Central Press*, "From the Centre Guards," July 12, 1861. In September 1861, Simmons was promoted to major of the 4th U.S. Infantry but opted to stay with the 5th Reserves. Ranks in the Regular Army were of more consequence than those in the temporary volunteer service, the latter established only for the duration of the war.

121. Bates, *Martial Deeds*, 408; Ellis, *Norwich University*, 222; Cullum, *Biographical Register*, 1:455.

122. Egle, *Notes and Queries*, 1:337–38. For a biography of Doyle—a native of Oconee County, Georgia, and a graduate from the Medical Department of the University of Pennsylvania in 1856—see Evans, *Confederate Military History*, 5:552–53. In his letter to Simmons's widow, Doyle wrote, "The impression I got of the name of your husband was 'Simons,' as if written

with one m. I suppose the reason of that was the weakness of his voice at the time." See Egle, *Notes and Queries*, 1:338.

123. *DT*, "The Realities of War," July 25, 1862; Joseph Fisher to Mrs. Seneca Simmons, July 21, 1862, Simmons Family Collection, HSDC.

124. Elmira Simmons Widow's Claim, Simmons Family Collection, HSDC.

125. *HT*, "Harrisburg in the Days of Civil War," October 3, 1905.

126. Moyer, *History of the Seventeenth Regiment*, 25–27; Regimental Association, *History of the Eighteenth Regiment*, 13, 34.

127. Moyer, *History of the Seventeenth Regiment*, 27; Mohr, *Cormany Diaries*, 247; Beidler, *Jacob Beidler's Book*, 135; Miller, *History of the 16th Regiment*, 35; Isaac H. Ressler Diary, November 10, 1862, *Civil War Times Illustrated Collection*, USAMHI.

128. Moyer, *History of the Seventeenth Regiment*, 27, 282–83, 322–24; Mohr, *Cormany Diaries*, 247; Beidler, *Jacob Beidler's Book*, 135; Ressler Diary, November 10, 1862, *Civil War Times Illustrated Collection*, USAMHI; Peter Boyer to Dear Father, November 20, 1862, Boyer Family Papers, HCWRT, USAMHI. The exact location of Camp McClellan remains a mystery. However, Private William Martin of the 18th Pennsylvania Cavalry (which would later join the 16th and 17th at Camp McClellan) wrote in a letter home on November 25, 1862, that "close by" Camp McClellan was "another camp…that is occupied by the militia[,] there are several thousand of them here." See Martin to Dear Wife, November 25, 1862, HCWRT, USAMHI. This camp "occupied by the militia," most likely referring to the 1862 Drafted Militia, is almost certainly Camp Simmons. This would place Camp McClellan a short distance north of Camp Simmons and roughly two miles north of the city, which concurs with the statement of several cavalrymen, including Private Peter Boyer of the 17th, who estimated in a November 20 letter to his father that Camp McClellan was located "about 2 miles from harrisburg." See Boyer to Dear Father, November 20, 1862, Boyer Family Papers, HCWRT, USAMHI. Additional details about Camp McClellan's location can be gleaned from a December 3, 1862 letter written by Martin in which he stated that the camp was situated "on high ground." In the same letter, Martin informed his wife that "we have to go through harrisburgh twice a day to water" the mounts. This would indicate that the camp was situated more at a northeasterly direction rather than directly north of Camp Simmons. See Martin to Dear Wife, December 3, 1862, HCWRT, USAMHI. Supporting this is the November 10 diary entry of Private Jacob Beidler

of the 16th, which places Camp McClellan "about 1½ miles northeast of Harrisburg." See Beidler, *Jacob Beidler's Book*, 135.

129. Regimental Association, *History of the Eighteenth Regiment*, 34; William H. Martin to Dear Wife, November 22, 25, 1862, HCWRT, USAMHI.

130. Moyer, *History of the Seventeenth Regiment*, 27; Mohr, *Cormany Diaries*, 250; Martin to Dear Wife, November 29, 1862, HCWRT, USAMHI; Boyer to Dear Father, November 20, 1862, Boyer Family Papers, HCWRT, USAMHI; *DT*, "The 17th Pennsylvania Cavalry and Its Commander," November 18, 1862.

131. Martin to Dear Wife, n.d., HCWRT, USAMHI.

132. Moyer, *History of the Seventeenth Regiment*, 28.

133. *DT*, "Unmanly Outrages," November 17, 1862.

134. Martin to Dear Wife, December 3, 1862, HCWRT, USAMHI.

135. Beidler, *Jacob Beidler's Book*, 136; Moyer, *History of the Seventeenth Regiment*, 27–28, 283; Martin to Dear Wife, December 3, 1862, HCWRT, USAMHI.

136. *DT*, "The Cavalrymen and Their Horses," November 24, 1862.

137. Ressler Diary, December 2–3, 1862, *Civil War Times Illustrated Collection*, USAMHI; Moyer, *History of the Seventeenth Regiment*, 29; Beidler, *Jacob Beidler's Book*, 137; *DT*, "Presentation of a Sword to Dr. James Moore," December 3, 1862.

138. Regimental Association, *History of the Eighteenth Regiment*, 34; Martin to Dear Wife, December 13, 1862, HCWRT, USAMHI.

139. Reuben Smeck Diary, July 28–31, 1863, Ronald D. Boyer Collection, USAMHI; *DPU*, "Camp Simmons," July 17, 1863; *DPU*, "Camps Curtin and Simmons," July 23, 1863. Also during the summer of 1863, "Strag's Camp" was established within the limits of Camp Curtin, with Captain Henry Chritzman, formerly of the 101st Pennsylvania, in charge. This sublet of Camp Curtin housed both deserters and stragglers, whom Chritzman fed in return for cleaning the encampment. See *DPU*, "Camps Curtin and Simmons," July 23, 1863.

140. Hewett, *Supplement to the Official Records*, 62:704.

141. Latta, *History of the First Regiment*, 80; *Philadelphia Press*, "The 'Gray Reserves,'" July 2, 1863.

142. *DT*, "Camp Haley," November 1, 1862; Bates, *History of Pennsylvania Volunteers*, 5:922, 1,324–25; *HT*, "Harrisburg in the Days of Civil War," October 3, 1905.

143. *DPU*, "New Regiment," March 3, 1863; *DPU*, "Camp Sands," March 6, 1863. One of the companies quartered in Camp Sands was Captain John B. Guthrie's unattached drafted militia company. With Pittsburgh

roots, Guthrie's men rendezvoused at Camp Howe near the steel city, where they remained through December 1862. Near the end of the year, Captain Guthrie and his company departed for Camp Curtin. On January 3—several days after their arrival at Curtin—the Pittsburghers were moved to Camp Sands, where they remained until February 23, when the outfit was relocated back to Camp Curtin. See Hewett, *Supplement to the Official Records*, 63:2, 519–20.

144. *ET*, "New Cavalry Camp," June 24, 1863; *ET*, "Chief of Cavalry," June 22, 1863; *DPU*, "Chief of Cavalry," June 23, 1863; *HT*, "Harrisburg in the Days of Civil War," October 3, 1905.

145. *ET*, "Camp 'Yahoo,'" June 20, 1863; Wingert, *Confederate Approach on Harrisburg*, 22–23.

146. Hewett, *Supplement to the Official Records*, 80:2, 27–33; *HT*, "Harrisburg in the Days of Civil War," October 3, 1905; *DT*, "Veterans," December 2, 1864.

147. Martin, *History of the Fifty-Seventh Regiment*, 161–62.

148. *The Globe*, "Local & Personal," June 7, 1865; Lewis Crater Diary, July 31–August 3, 1865, Special Collections, University of Iowa. On July 31, the *Philadelphia Press* reported, "Nearly all the troops recently at Camp Return, Harrisburg, have been paid off, and returned to their homes." See *Philadelphia Press*, "State Items," July 31, 1865.

Life in Camp Curtin

149. Brandt, *Mr. Tubbs' Civil War*, 9, 13–15.

150. *Harrisburg Evening News*, "Old Camp Curtin," October 20, 1922. Matchette was interviewed while attending the Curtin Memorial dedication in 1922.

151. Walters, "Off to the War," HCWRT, USAMHI.

152. Alexander, *126ᵗʰ Pennsylvania*, 107–8.

153. George McFarland to Dear Wife, September 28, 1862, George McFarland Papers, J. Horace McFarland Papers, MG 85, Pennsylvania State Archives.

154. Bloodgood, *Personal Reminiscences of the War*, 14–15.

155. Rice, "Memoir," 31, 78–79, Nicholas Rice Papers, USAMHI. Rice later recalled Camp Curtin as the "ground where I had been initiated into the duties of a soldier."

156. *Democratic Banner*, "Letter from Camp," September 10, 1862.

157. Davis, *History of the Doylestown Guards*, 104.

158. Albert, *History of the Forty-Fifth Regiment*, 224.

159. Ibid., 265.

160. Beebe to Mother, October 17, 1862, and Beebe to P.J., October 22, 1862, CWD, USAMHI.

161. Brandt, *Mr. Tubbs' Civil War*, 9, 13–15.

162. Albert, *History of the Forty-Fifth Regiment*, 263–64.

163. Alexander, *126th Pennsylvania*, 109–10.

164. Ibid., 107–10; Bloodgood, *Personal Reminiscences of the War*, 15; Albert, *History of the Forty-Fifth Regiment*, 264–65.

165. Beebe to P.J., October 22, 1862, and Beebe to Mother, October 17, 1862, CWD, USAMHI.

166. Albert, *History of the Forty-Fifth Regiment*, 265; Richards, *History of Company C*, 18; Parker, *History of the 51st*, 20–22.

167. Castleman, *Army of the Potomac*, 7–8.

168. Brandt, *Mr. Tubbs' Civil War*, 9, 15–16.

169. Ibid., 10.

170. Parker, *History of the 51st*, 16–18.

171. Kerr, *Civil War Surgeon*, 22.

172. Parker, *History of the 51st*, 24–25.

173. "Smith" to "Friend Black," August 17, 1862, MG 7, Pennsylvania State Archives.

174. Ibid.; Parker, *History of the 51st*, 25; *DT*, "The Camps," November 14, 1861.

175. *The Agitator*, "From Captain Merrick's Company," July 22, 1863.

176. *DPU*, "Camp Curtin," April 24, 1861.

177. *Philadelphia Press*, "Letter from Harrisburg," August 20, 1862.

178. Rumsey, *Mansfield Men*, 19.

179. Parker, *History of the 51st*, 19–20.

180. Smith, "Memoirs of Francis M. Smith," GNMP.

181. Parker, *History of the 51st*, 25.

182. Sprenger, *Concise History*, 322.

183. Walters, "Off to the War," HCWRT, USAMHI; Henry F. Charles Memoir, Ronald D. Boyer Collection, USAMHI.

184. Charles Memoir, Boyer Collection, USAMHI; Welsh, "Some Personal Experience," W.S. Nye Papers, GNMP; Smith, "Memoirs of Francis M. Smith," GNMP.

185. *Democratic Banner*, "Letter from a Soldier," October 12, 1863; Baker to Dear Mother, October 28, 1861, and Baker to Folks at Home, December 7, 1861, GNMP.

186. Eli Strouss to Dear Friend, October 21, 1861, *Civil War Times Illustrated Collection*, USAMHI.

187. Baker to Dear Mother, October 28, 1861, GNMP; Albert, *History of the Forty-Fifth Regiment*, 264.

188. Beebe to Dear Respected Wife and Children, November 12, 1862, CWD, USAMHI.

189. Luther Granger to Old Woman, November 11, 1862, CWD, USAMHI.

190. Parker, *History of the 51ˢᵗ*, 12.

191. Granger to Dear Wife, n.d., CWD, USAMHI.

192. *The Agitator*, "News from the Tioga Boys," July 3, 1861.

193. Craft, *History of the One Hundred Forty-First Regiment*, 9.

194. Zorn, *Sergeant's Story*, 19; "Smith" to "Friend Black."

195. Jonathan W. Kerr Diary, June 1–3, 1865, MG 6, Pennsylvania State Archives.

196. Pennypacker, "Six Weeks in Uniform," 395–96.

197. Mohr, *Cormany Diaries*, 578–79.

198. Strouss to Dear Friend, October 21, 1861, *Civil War Times Illustrated Collection*, USAMHI.

199. McCalmont, *Extracts from Letters*, 73, 85, 87–92.

200. Ibid., 93–99.

201. Craft, *History of the One Hundred and Forty-First Regiment*, 9.

202. Moyer, *History of the Seventeenth Regiment*, 282–83.

Civilian-Soldier Interaction in Harrisburg

203. Smith, "Memoirs of Francis M. Smith," GNMP.

204. *DT*, "Unmanly Outrages," November 17, 1862.

205. Smith, "Memoirs of Francis M. Smith," GNMP.

206. Book, *Northern Rendezvous*, 57; *DT*, "The Harrisburg Hospital," December 17, 1862.

207. *DT*, "The Cotton Mill," June 18, 1861; Morgan, *Annals of Harrisburg*, 416; Henry Gerrish Memoir, *Civil War Times Illustrated Collection*, USAMHI.

208. Morgan, *Annals of Harrisburg*, 416; Kelker, *History of Dauphin County*, 1:539; miscellaneous newspaper clippings, German Scrapbook, HSDC. The East Walnut Street hospital had been located in a schoolhouse on Walnut Street since early October 1862 and was closed on March 23, 1863, with its patients removed to the hospitals at Camp Curtin and the Cotton Factory. Shortly after the patients had departed, the school was "fitted up for re-occupation by the north ward male schools." In all likelihood, this hospital was in the Lancastrian schoolhouse, the same location of the East Walnut Street Hospital in operation during the summer of 1863. See *DPU*, "Evacuated," March 24, 1863; *DT*, "Perilous Leap," October 4, 1862.

209. *DPU*, "East Walnut Street Hospital," August 31, 1863.

210. *DPU*, "Our Schools," September 30, 1863.

211. Morgan, *Annals of Harrisburg*, 416, 443; Kelker, *History of Dauphin County*, 1:539.

212. Kelker, *History of Dauphin County*, 1:539; *DT*, "The Ladies," October 6, 1862; *DPU*, "Proscription," October 9, 1863.

213. *The Agitator*, "From Captain Merrick's Company," September 16, 1863.

214. "Smith" to "Friend Black."

215. *DT*, "We Learn," August 16, 1862.

216. Matthews, *The 149th Pennsylvania*, 36.

217. *Philadelphia Press*, "Letter from Harrisburg," August 20, 1862.

218. *Central Press*, "From Camp Curtin," May 9, 1861.

COPPERHEAD CAPITAL

219. Pennypacker, "Six Weeks in Uniform," 313.

220. Book, *Northern Rendezvous*, 80–82; *DPU*, "Democratic City Nominations," March 16, 1863; *New York Times*, "Death of General Roumfort," August 3, 1878.

221. Book, *Northern Rendezvous*, 81–82; *DPU*, "Great Democratic Victory" and "The City Election," March 21, 1863.

222. *DT*, "A Wonderful Discovery," April 12, 1862; *DT*, "How to Recognize a K.G.C.," October 21, 1861.

223. Pennypacker, "Six Weeks in Uniform," 311–13.
224. *ET*, "How the Copperhead Convention Treats Union Soldiers," June 19, 1863.

Harrisburg and the Gettysburg Campaign

225. *Philadelphia Daily Evening Bulletin*, "Accounts by Mail From Harrisburg," June 17, 1863.
226. This essay discusses the city of Harrisburg during the Maryland and Gettysburg Campaigns. The focus of this study is primarily activities and reactions from inside the city of Harrisburg. For a more detailed account covering the actions during the Gettysburg Campaign in Harrisburg and neighboring Cumberland County, see the author's previous title, *The Confederate Approach on Harrisburg*.
227. *Official Records*, 27:3, 914.
228. *DT*, "Proclamation," September 12, 1862.
229. Kelker, *History of Dauphin County*, 3:22; Egle et al., *Commemorative Biographical Encyclopedia*, 338; "Campaign of the First Regiment," newspaper clippings, McCormick Family Papers, MG 466, HSDC; reminiscence by unidentified soldier, Brooks-Bigler Family Papers, Cumberland County Historical Society; H.D. Murray to Dear Sister, September 18, 1862, Cumberland County Historical Society. While in the field, McCormick was promoted to brigadier general and placed in command of a brigade of militia.
230. *DT*, "The State Capital Full of New Levies," September 15, 1862.
231. Charles Memoir, Boyer Collection, USAMHI.
232. *Pittsburg Daily Gazette and Advertiser*, "From Harrisburg," September 15, 1862. Riddle's company was later designated Company B, 15th Pennsylvania Militia.
233. Wister, *Jones Wister's Reminiscences*, 152–53.
234. *DT*, "The Troops in the Capital," September 16, 1862.
235. John F. Reynolds to My Dear Sisters, September 28, 1862, Eleanor Reynolds Scrapbook, Reynolds Family Papers, Franklin and Marshall College Archives; *DT*, "The State Capital Full of New Levies," September 15, 1862.
236. Miscellaneous newspaper clippings, German Scrapbook, HSDC.

237. *Official Records*, 27:2, 211–12.

238. *DPU*, "The Feeling Yesterday," June 15, 1863.

239. *ET*, "War Meeting," June 15, 1863; *DPU*, "Meeting of Citizens," June 15, 1863.

240. Wingert, *Confederate Approach on Harrisburg*, 26–28; Gottschalk, *Notes*, 210; *Philadelphia Daily Evening Bulletin*, "Harrisburg in Danger," June 16, 1863; *Philadelphia Daily Evening Bulletin*, "Accounts by Mail From Harrisburg," June 17, 1863; *New York Tribune*, "Harrisburg," June 17, 1863; *HT*, "Harrisburg in the Days of Civil War," October 3, 1905; *DPU*, "Fearful Accident," June 17, 1863.

241. Gottschalk, *Notes*, 209–12.

242. *Philadelphia Daily Evening Bulletin*, "Accounts by Mail From Harrisburg," June 17, 1863; *Philadelphia Press*, "Great Gathering at the Capital," June 17, 1863.

243. R. Went Diary, June 16–17, 1863, MG 6, Pennsylvania State Archives.

244. *Philadelphia Daily Evening Bulletin*, "Accounts from Harrisburg by Mail," June 18, 1863.

245. Ibid., June 19, 1863.

246. Jacob R. Spangler to Dear Mother, June 18, 1863, Strokes L. Roberts Papers, MG 198, Pennsylvania State Archives.

247. Wingate, *History of the Twenty-Second*, 175.

248. *DPU*, "War Meeting Yesterday Morning," June 17, 1863; William B. Franklin to William F. Smith, June 23, 1863, Smith Papers, Vermont Historical Society.

249. Lockwood, *Our Campaign*, 23.

250. Wingate, *History of the Twenty-Second*, 169–70.

251. Pennypacker, "Six Weeks in Uniform," 312.

252. *ET*, "Cavalry Men, Attention!," June 15, 1863.

253. *HT*, "Harrisburg in the Days of Civil War," October 3, 1905.

254. Ibid.; *ET*, "The Situation," July 1, 1863.

HARRISBURG AFTER THE CIVIL WAR

255. *Philadelphia Daily Evening Bulletin*, "Winding up Affairs at Camp Curtin," November 15, 1865, quoting the *Telegraph*.

256. Ibid.

257. Williams, *Ceremonies at the Dedication*, 8–9.
258. Miscellaneous newspaper clippings, German Scrapbook, HSDC.
259. Wister, *Jones Wister's Reminiscences*, 180.
260. Steinmetz and Hoffsommer, *This Was Harrisburg*, 101.
261. Williams, *Ceremonies at the Dedication*, 18–23.
262. Steinmetz and Hoffsommer, *This Was Harrisburg*, 48; Inglewood, *Then and Now in Harrisburg*, 82–85, 155.

Bibliography

BOOKS

Albert, Allen, ed. *History of the Forty-Fifth Regiment Pennsylvania Veteran Volunteer Infantry 1861–1865*. Williamsport, PA: Grit Publishing Company, 1912.

Alexander, Ted, ed. *The 126ᵗʰ Pennsylvania*. Shippensburg, PA: Beidel Printing House, 1984.

Bates, Samuel. *History of Pennsylvania Volunteers, 1861–5*. 5 vols. Harrisburg, PA: B. Singerly, State Printer, 1869–71.

———. *Martial Deeds of Pennsylvania*. Philadelphia: T.H. Davis & Company, 1876.

Beidler, Jacob. *Jacob Beidler's Book No. A: A Diary Kept by Jacob Beidler from November 1857 thru July 1863*. Edited by Robert Winder. Mifflintown, PA: Juniata County Historical Society, 1994.

Bloodgood, J.D. *Personal Reminiscences of the War*. New York: Hunt & Eaton, 1893.

Book, Janet Mae. *Northern Rendezvous: Harrisburg During the Civil War*. Harrisburg, PA: Telegraph Press, 1951.

Brandt, Nat. *Mr. Tubbs' Civil War*. Syracuse, NY: Syracuse University Press, 1996.

Bush, James C. *A Short History of the Fifth Regiment U.S. Artillery*. Governors Island, NY, 1895.

Castleman, Alfred L. *The Army of the Potomac Behind the Scenes: A Diary of Unwritten History*. Milwaukee, WI: Strickland and Company, 1863.

Chamberlin, David. *Cleaning Up the Muss: The Civil War Letters of Surgeon David P. Chamberlin to the Hudson Gazette Newspaper*. Edited by Marty Bertera and Hazel Pray Monahan. Newport: Vermont Civil War Enterprises, 2007.

Cornwallis, Kinahan. *Royalty in the New World; or the Prince of Wales in America*. New York: M. Doolady, 1860.

Craft, David. *History of the One Hundred Forty-First Regiment, Pennsylvania Volunteers, 1862–1865*. Towanda, PA: Reporter-Journal Printing, 1885.

Cullum, George. *Biographical Register of the Officers and Graduates of the U.S. Military Academy at West Point, N.Y., from Its Establishment, March 16, 1802 to the Army Reorganization of 1866–1867*. 2 vols. New York: D. Van Nostrand, 1868.

Davis, William W.H. *History of the Doylestown Guards*. 2 vols. Doylestown, PA: Democrat Job Department, 1887.

Dickens, Charles. *American Notes for General Circulation*. London: Chapman and Hall, 1842.

Dornblaser, Thomas. *My Life Story for Young and Old*. Published for the author, 1930.

———. *Sabre Strokes of the Pennsylvania Dragoons in the War of 1861–1865*. Philadelphia: Lutheran Publication Society, 1884.

Eggert, Gerald. *Harrisburg Industrializes: The Coming of Factories to an American Community*. University Park: Pennsylvania State University Press, 1993.

Egle, William Henry. *Notes and Queries: Historical, Biographical and Genealogical Relating Chiefly to Interior Pennsylvania*. 12 vols. Harrisburg, PA: Harrisburg Publishing Company, 1894–1901.

Egle, William Henry et al. *Commemorative Biographical Encyclopedia of Dauphin County, Pennsylvania…*. Chambersburg, PA: J.M. Runk & Company, 1896.

Ellis, William Arba, ed. *Norwich University 1819–1911: Her History, Her Graduates, Her Roll of Honor*. 3 vols. Montpelier, VT: Capital City Press, 1911.

Evans, Clement Anselm, ed. *Confederate Military History: A Library of Confederate States History…*. 12 vols. Atlanta, GA: Confederate Publishing Company, 1899.

Gansevoort, Henry Sanford. *Memorial of Henry Sanford Gansevoort*. Edited by J.C. Hoadley. Boston: Franklin Press, 1875.

Glazier, Willard. *Peculiarities of American Cities*. Philadelphia: Hubbard Brothers, 1886.

Gottschalk, Louis Moreau. *Notes of a Pianist: During His Professional Tours in the United States, Canada, the Antilles, and South America*. London: J.B. Lippincott, 1881.

Heitman, Francis. *Historical Register and Dictionary of the United States Army, from Its Organization, September 29, 1789, to March 2, 1903*. 2 vols. Washington, D.C.: Government Printing Office, 1903.

Holmes, Oliver Wendell. *Pages from an Old Volume of Life: A Collection of Essays 1857–1881*. Boston: Houghton, Mifflin and Company, 1889.

Inglewood, Marian. *Then and Now in Harrisburg*. Harrisburg, PA, 1925.

Kelker, Luther Reily. *History of Dauphin County, Pennsylvania*. 3 vols. New York: Lewis Publishing Company, 1907.

Kerr, Paul. *Civil War Surgeon: Biography of James Langstaff Dunn, MD*. Bloomington, IN: AuthorHouse, 2005.

Latta, James William. *History of the First Regiment Infantry National Guard of Pennsylvania (Gray Reserves) 1861–1911*. Philadelphia: J.B. Lippincott Company, 1912.

Lockwood, John. *Our Campaign Around Gettysburg*. Brooklyn, NY: A.H. Rome and Brothers, 1864.

Lossing, Benson. *Memoir of Lieut.-Col. John T. Greble of the United States Army*. Philadelphia: privately printed, 1870.

Lucas, Thomas. *I Seat Myself to Write You a Few Lines: Civil War and Homestead Letters from Thomas Lucas and Family*. Edited by Thomas Lucas Bayard and Dona Bayard Sauerburger. Bowie, MD: Heritage Books, 2002.

Martin, James. *History of the Fifty-Seventh Regiment, Pennsylvania Veteran Volunteer Infantry…*. Meadville, PA: McCoy and Calvin, 1904.

Matthews, Richard. *The 149th Pennsylvania Volunteer Infantry Unit in the Civil War*. Jefferson, NC: McFarland and Company, 1994.

McCalmont, Alfred. *Extracts from Letters Written by Alfred B. McCalmont from the Front During the War of the Rebellion*. Franklin, PA: printed for private circulation by Robert McCalmont, 1908.

McClure, A.K. *Abraham Lincoln and Men of War Times: Some Personal Recollections of War and Politics During the Lincoln Administration*. Philadelphia: Times Publishing Company, 1892.

Miller, Charles. *History of the 16th Regiment Pennsylvania Cavalry, For the Year Ending October 31st, 1863*. Philadelphia: King and Baird Printers, 1864.

Mohr, James C., ed. *The Cormany Diaries: A Northern Family in the Civil War*. Pittsburgh, PA: University of Pittsburgh Press, 1982.

Molyneux, Joel. *Quill of the Wild Goose: Civil War Letters and Diaries of Private Joel Molyneux, 141st P.V.* Edited by Kermit Molyneux Bird. Shippensburg, PA: Burd Street Press, 1996.

Montgomery, Morton. *Historical and Biographical Annals of Berks County Pennsylvania*. 2 vols. Chicago: J.H. Beers & Company, 1909.

Morgan, George. *Annals of Harrisburg: Comprising Memoirs, Incidents and Statistics from the Period of Its First Settlement*. Harrisburg, PA: Evangelical Publishing House, 1906.

Moyer, H.P. *History of the Seventeenth Regiment Pennsylvania Volunteer Cavalry or One Hundred and Sixty-Second in the Line of Pennsylvania Volunteer Regiments*. Lebanon, PA: Sowers Printing Company, 1911.

Muffly, J.W., ed. *The Story of Our Regiment: A History of the 148th Pennsylvania Vols*. Des Moines, IA: Kenyon Printing & MGF Company, 1904.

Parker, Thomas. *History of the 51st Regiment of P.V. and V.V.* Philadelphia: King & Baird, Printers, 1869.

Porter, John. *76th Regiment Pennsylvania Volunteer Infantry Keystone Zouaves: The Personal Recollections 1861–1865 of Sergeant John A. Porter Company "B."* Edited by James Chisman. Wilmington, NC: Broadfoot Publishing Company, 1988.

Regimental Association. *History of the Eighteenth Regiment of Cavalry Pennsylvania Volunteers (163d Regiment of the Line) 1862–1865*. New York: Wynkoop, Hallenback, Crawford Company, 1909.

———. *History of the 127th Regiment Pennsylvania Volunteers, Familiarly Known as the "Dauphin County Regiment."* Lebanon, PA: Report Publishing Company, circa 1902.

Richards, J. Stuart. *A History of Company C, 50th Pennsylvania Veteran Volunteer Infantry Regiment: From the Camp, the Battlefield and the Prison Pen, 1861–1865*. London: The History Press, 2006.

Rowell, John. *Yankee Cavalrymen: Through the Civil War with the Ninth Pennsylvania Cavalry*. Knoxville: University of Tennessee Press, 1971.

Rumsey, Charles. *Mansfield Men in the Seventh Pennsylvania Cavalry, Eightieth Regiment, with Letters of Charles M. Rumsey and Personal War Sketches, 1861–1865*. Edited by Chester P. Bailey. Mansfield, PA: Chester P. Bailey, 1986.

Sprenger, George. *Concise History of the Camp and Field Life of the 122d Regiment Penn'a Volunteers…*. Lancaster, PA: New Era Stream Book Print, 1885.

Steinmetz, Richard, and Robert Hoffsommer. *This Was Harrisburg: A Photographic History*. Harrisburg, PA: Stackpole Books, 1976.

Thompson, Heber. *The First Defenders*. N.p., 1910.

Trussell, John B.B. "Brig. Gen. Joseph F. Knipe, U.S.V." Unpublished manuscript, Pennsylvania Historical and Museum Commission, 1980.

Warner, Ezra. *Generals in Blue: Lives of the Union Commanders*. Baton Rouge: Louisiana State University, 1964.

Washington, George. *President Washington's Diaries: 1791 to 1799*. Compiled by Joseph Hoskins. Summerfield, NC, 1921.

Williams, Alvin. *Ceremonies at the Dedication of the Statue of Andrew Gregg Curtin War Governor of Pennsylvania.* Harrisburg, PA: Telegraph Printing Company, 1922.

Wingate, George. *History of the Twenty-Second Regiment of the National Guard of the State of New York: From Its Organization to 1895.* New York: E.W. Dayton, 1896.

Wingert, Cooper. *The Confederate Approach on Harrisburg: The Gettysburg Campaign's Northernmost Reaches.* Charleston, SC: The History Press, 2012.

Wister, Jones. *Jones Wister's Reminiscences.* Philadelphia: J.B. Lippincott, 1920.

Zorn, Jacob. *A Sergeant's Story: Civil War Diary of Jacob J. Zorn, 1862–1865.* Edited by Barbara Croner. Apolla, PA: Closson Press, 1999.

OFFICIAL DOCUMENTS

Hewett, Janet B., ed. *Supplement to the Official Records of the Union and Confederate Armies.* 100 vols. Wilmington, NC: Broadfoot Publishing Company, 1994–2004.

U.S. War Department. *The War of the Rebellion: A Compilation of the Official Records of the Union and Confederate Armies.* 128 vols. Washington, D.C.: Government Printing Office, 1880–1901.

ARTICLES AND PERIODICALS

Pennypacker, Samuel. "Six Weeks in Uniform." *Historical and Biographical Sketches.* Philadelphia: Robert Tripple, 1883.

NEWSPAPERS

The Agitator, Wellsboro, Pennsylvania, 1854–65.
Altoona Tribune, Altoona, Pennsylvania, 1856–19??.

Central Press, Bellefonte, Pennsylvania, 1858–68.

Daily Patriot and Union, Harrisburg, Pennsylvania, 1858–68.

Daily Pittsburgh Gazette and Commercial Journal, Pittsburgh, Pennsylvania, 1861–63.

Daily Telegraph and *Evening Telegraph*, Harrisburg, Pennsylvania, 1831–1948.

Danville Intelligencer, Danville, Pennsylvania, 1859–1907.

Democratic Banner, Clearfield, Pennsylvania, 183?–1???.

The Globe, Huntingdon, Pennsylvania, 1856–77.

New York Times, New York, 1851–present.

Philadelphia Daily Evening Bulletin, Philadelphia, Pennsylvania, 1856–70.

Philadelphia Press, Philadelphia, Pennsylvania, 1857–80.

MANUSCRIPTS

CUMBERLAND COUNTY HISTORICAL SOCIETY, HAMILTON LIBRARY, CARLISLE, PENNSYLVANIA:
Brooks-Bigler Family Papers.
   "Reminisce by Unidentified Soldier."
H.D. Murray to Dear Sister, September 18, 1862.

FRANKLIN AND MARSHALL COLLEGE ARCHIVES, LANCASTER, PENNSYLVANIA:
Eleanor Reynolds Scrapbook.
   John F. Reynolds to My Dear Sisters, September 28, 1862.

GETTYSBURG NATIONAL MILITARY PARK LIBRARY, GETTYSBURG, PENNSYLVANIA:
Francis Smith. "Memoirs of Francis M. Smith."
Isaac R. Dunkelberger. "Reminiscences and Personal Experiences of the Great Rebellion."
Joseph Baker Letters.
Robert Welsh. "Some Personal Experience." Wilbur S. Nye Papers.

HISTORICAL SOCIETY OF DAUPHIN COUNTY, ALEXANDER FAMILY LIBRARY, HARRISBURG, PENNSYLVANIA:
Manuscript Group 275, Simmons Family Collection.
   Elmira Simmons. "Reminiscence of My Childhood."
   Genealogy document.

Joseph Fisher to Mrs. Seneca Simmons, July 21, 1862.
  Widow's Claim, Elmira Simmons.
Manuscript Group 466, McCormick Family Collection.
  Newspaper clippings, "Campaign of the First Regiment."
Philip German Scrapbook.

PENNSYLVANIA STATE ARCHIVES, PENNSYLVANIA HISTORIC AND MUSEUM
    COMMISSION, HARRISBURG, PENNSYLVANIA:
Manuscript Group 6, Diaries and Journals Collection.
  Jonathan Kerr Diary.
  R. Went Diary.
Manuscript Group 7, Military Manuscripts Collection.
  "Smith" to "Friend Black," August 17, 1862.
Manuscript Group 85, J. Horace McFarland Papers.
  George McFarland Letters.
Manuscript Group 198, Strokes L. Roberts Papers.
  Jacob Spangler to Dear Mother, June 18, 1863

UNIVERSITY OF IOWA, SPECIAL COLLECTIONS, IOWA CITY, IOWA:
Lewis Crater Diary.

UNIVERSITY OF MICHIGAN, BENTLEY HISTORICAL LIBRARY, ANN ARBOR, MICHIGAN:
Edward H.C. Taylor to My Dear Sister, June 31, 1861.
J.D. Richardson to Unspecified, June 28, 1861.
John Milton Bancroft Diary.

U.S. ARMY MILITARY HISTORY INSTITUTE, CARLISLE BARRACKS, CARLISLE,
    PENNSYLVANIA:
Civil War Document Collection.
  Benjamin Steiner to Dear Brother, October 18, 1861.
  Charles Pollock to Dear Ma, April 19, 1861.
  Graham Family Papers.
  Joseph Higgins Letters.
  Luther Granger Letters.
  Lyman Beebe Letters.
  Orbo W. Palmer to Dear Sister, December 7, 1861.
  Samuel J. Alexander Letters.
Civil War Times Illustrated Collection.
  Eli Strouss to Dear Friend, October 21, 1861.

Henry Gerrish Memoir.
Isaac H. Ressler Diary.
George Miller Papers.
John J. Miller to Dear Brother, November 28, 1861.
Harrisburg Civil War Roundtable Collection.
Bently Kutz Diary.
Edgar A. Walters. "Off to the War: A Year in the Ranks."
Peter Boyer to Dear Father, November 20, 1862.
William H. Martin Letters.
Nicholas Rice Papers.
Nicholas Rice "Memoir."
Pardee-Robinson Collection.
Calvin Pardee to Dear Pa, April 18, 1861.
Ronald D. Boyer Collection.
Henry F. Charles Memoir.
Reuben Smeck Diary.

VERMONT HISTORICAL SOCIETY, LEAHY LIBRARY, BARRE, VERMONT:
William F. Smith Papers.
William Franklin to William F. Smith, June 23, 1863.

Index

About the Author

Cooper Wingert is a south-central Pennsylvania student who has authored and edited numerous books and articles on the Gettysburg Campaign and Harrisburg's role in the Civil War. He regularly speaks to area Civil War round tables, historical societies and other groups.

Visit us online at:
www.historypress.net